MW01289800

the past to Freedom
el pasado a la Libertad

by Jeremy Michael Vasquez
Jeremías Miguel Vasquez

Other books by Jeremy Michael Vasquez:

Bold, Assertive & Tender

Unshackled

*These books are available at quantity discounts
with bulk purchase for educational use.
For more information, contact the author at
jeremymichaelvasquez@gmail.com.*

*In order to support the struggle for freedom and
the fight for immigrants' rights, 10% of all book
sales will be donated directly to the Bay Area
Chapter of Border Angels. Find out more about
the work this organization is doing to save lives
and make a difference at borderangels.org.*

By purchasing this book,
you are an agent of change.

Jeremy Michael Vasquez is an artist, author, healer and educator in San Francisco. He uses his expression of art to facilitate healing workshops in a variety of settings across the country. These workshops are interactive and come from an Afro-Latino teaching pedagogy where there is movement, vibration and high energy. Subjects such as identity, mental health, and toxic masculinity are explored. As a spoken word and musical artist, he has performed at many community events as well as educational and correctional facilities. Serving as a keynote speaker at conferences, colleges, universities, and public schools nationwide, Jeremy continues to use his pain as a platform for change. With his poetry, he has been called to free people through storytelling.

Contents

Dedication

"Señor. Señor."
The young children say to me,
Tugging on my Mexican poncho.
I pull out some pesos from my pocket and drop
them generously on the same table we had
previously interlocked oddly-shaped jigsaws
together. Puzzled when I will return. I know
when I leave the volunteer shelter in Tijuana,
Mexico they will never see me again.

I don't want to be just 'another' visitor
who comes to their home, leaving blankets and
sweets. I want to enhance their self-esteem. I
want to reduce their anxiety. But most
importantly, I want them to feel like 'kids again.'
Not refugees, asylum seekers or migrants. Not
political pawns in the crossfire of a nation on the
brink of war. But the bushy-tailed, bright-eyed
younger versions of ourselves that just want to
dance under the waterfall of a fire hydrant.

So I lift them into the air like the angels
they are, put them on my shoulders, swing them
around. Push them on swings, play soccer and
basketball with them, and chase them around
the park. Their giggles provide all the reciprocity
I could ever ask for. When it is time to kiss them
goodbye after an unforgettable week, I hear a
voice squeak...

"Recuérdame." Remember Me. It is one of
the boys that summer who took a liking to
me. Held my hand when we crossed the streets.
Clenched his jaw to prevent his lips from

trembling whenever I tucked him in his tent while I went back to my 5 star hotel. I could tell by the grip he had during our final hug what he was involuntarily saying. I did not need to speak Spanish to understand his body language. I weep the whole taxi ride back to the border.

He did not know "Remember Me" was the title of a song to one of my favorite movies, COCO. Which till this day, still makes me cry my eyes out. He does not know that even if I tried, I could never forget him with all he and his family were going through. And all he did not know was awaiting him in America...

I'm wrapping up a healing workshop which ties the concepts of cultural identity and youth empowerment together months later in Santa Ana, California. The students are a blessing to work with. Young, gifted and brown. Their teacher who specializes in radical self-care has given birth to inquisitive scholars who like her, know how to advocate for themselves.

It is the oldest and largest high school in a notoriously conservative Orange County. The enrollment at Santa Ana High School is 99% Latino. 1 in 4 students is learning English as a second language. The poverty rate is 86%. I am 100% confident I am exactly where I need to be.

"I wish you here about a week ago." One of the students mutters under their breath. Whispers quickly ensue. I come from families that sweep the transgressions of its members under the carpet, so it takes no time to come to the conclusion there are skeletons in this closet. In between a rock and a hard place, I have to choose to open Pandora's box or ignore that signal of distress. I ask what happened. My question met with a deafening silence. A brave voice arose from the shame, and though trembling, she said:

"There was a football game last week. It was the red/white/blue game we have every year since 9/11. There were signs in the stadium that read 'We're gonna TRUMP YOU.' 'We love white.' There were chants of 'BUILD A WALL' and 'Go back to Mexico' after every touchdown. Some people threw taco shells on the players from their seats. When I got home I couldn't sleep. They thought they were playing against animals, not kids who live 20 minutes down the freeway. It was out of control. I have never been that afraid before."

Tears rolled down her face like a bike pedaling downhill. Her avalanche of pain in full display. I want to suck the poison out of her, but the venom has spread through her lymphatic system. This underscored the broader tension an entire people are facing. I see headstrong teenagers retract themselves in the blink of an eye. I witness firsthand the intersectionality of hateful rhetoric and terrorizing acts.

I asked the teacher, what's next? She says lunch. I jot down a question in my passion planner after the bell rings. Some food for thought. *When we bleed patriotism from our veins, what do we do with all the blood on our hands?*

I open a fortune cookie at home during dinner. I do not know the chances of getting the same message twice. But I get the memo loud and clear the first time. I put it on the back of my phone case, besides the photo of my daughter to be reminded of what I'm fighting for. It reads: 'Human rights. Know them. Demand them. Defend them.'

A week later I am at a dinner table in Mi-Wuk village. Up in the snowy mountains of the Bay Area having a heated race-relation conversation over dinner fresh outta the oven, washed down with bottles of refrigerated wine. Just a little something to hold us together for Thanksgiving.

I am thankful to have a home, food to eat, and clean water, which is more than a lot of people can say. The family around the table was not afforded to me at birth, but supplied to me in good faith. Without WiFi I am disconnected from the horrors of society, but when I return to civilization, I am unaware of the immaculate conception awaiting me.

Images of children, barefoot in diapers, being tear gassed at the border greet me. After a year filled with deplorable and inhumane acts of aggression, this is the straw that broke the camel's back. America with our Starbucks coffee, subsidized Chiquita bananas, and cheap labor by way of U.S intervention in Central America, struck a match in me. And it would take more than bombs, bullets and tear gas to snuff out the candle.

In numerous parts of the world this year, I have witnessed a trend: the same suffering of those who look just like me. If you want to see how good we're doing as a people, look at our youth.

The Latin phrase 'omne trium perfectum' (everything that comes in 3s is perfect) was the only confirmation I needed to begin this, the final book of my trilogy.

If we do nothing, neither are we.

This is dedicated to anyone who ever read the diary of Anne Frank and thought, what would I do? Or read the Hunger Games and wanted to follow the Mockingjay. Or who believes an injustice anywhere is a threat to justice everywhere. If you still believe humanity is worth fighting for, do not look further.

Now is the time.

Acknowledgments

I want to acknowledge a young girl named Karen who approached me an Ethnic studies summit at Chapman University in Southern California. After listening to me perform, she asked me to speak to her high school. At the time, I was unaware she would open doors to new windows of opportunities, or that her single act of courage would set off a chain reaction for the remainder of the year.

For every young woman of color–who like Karen–stood in line, anxious with clammy hands, patiently waiting for the invitation to my altar call. Who after listening to my spoken word, recognized the brokenness in me and found sanctuary in my house of blues. Who had limited heart to hearts which felt more like confessions than conversations. Who felt compelled enough to put down their shield and pour themselves empty onto the shoulders of a complete stranger. Who for once, didn't have to wipe their own tears.

Because all too familiarly the voices of young girls are driven 'underground.' And as they lose their distinctive ability to vocalize themselves during adolescence, we too are deprived of their healthy resistance until they later resurface in their womanhood to reclaim their strong female voice. I don't blame them for their confliction. I have met too many young girls fighting silent battles.

Apologies they are owed and those that might never be delivered, but the most important by far are the ones they owe to themselves. For ever thinking they are not worthy. Or enough. When in reality, everything they need already exists within them. It takes women too many years to unlearn what they have been taught to be sorry about. In the creation of this book, I want to acknowledge their magic, which in every setting I'm in, will never ever go unnoticed.

For the past two years since the release of my second book, *Unshackled,* I have been without a permanent residence, but I have resided in the hearts of my community, and have been dependent on the kindness of others. As I have experienced the plights of my father firsthand, I've learned how intertwined we all are, and how one person's struggles can affect an entire village.

If you have ever given me a couch to sleep on, a pillow to rest my head, a warm meal to feed my soul, or any other kind of sustenance, I am eternally grateful and indebted to you. The fear of not knowing where you're going to sleep at night is something I wish on nobody. It is my hope that this body of work will help to inspire someone to keep going and show that you can still be an agent of change even while you are in the midst of your own personal chaos.

May you reconcile your pain within and come to your own innerstanding on the past to Freedom.

For Nahla

House full of women

I was raised in a house full of women
That were head of the household.
That held the foundation
Together like a backbone.
It is because of them
I learned how to think on my own two feet.
Their feet, usually swollen
From working double shifts
Those feet, usually swollen
Picking up graveyard hours.
So I,
The child they adopted
Could live a normal life
Learning lessons
On organized sports teams.

I was raised in a house full of women
Who attended every soccer game
I ever laced my cleats in.
Who sliced those oranges every weekend.
Who went bananas when I split the defense.
Who iced my wounds after every practice.
Who hoisted me on shoulders
When I scored a game winning goal.
Their goal–prepare this Afro-Latino
For life in America.
Their goal–prepare me for
High pressure moments.

I was raised in a house full of women
Who told me at an early age:
Jeremy, you are way different.
You're gonna have to work twice,
Three times as hard as everybody else.
Excuses will not live here.
Your st..st..st..t.ttt.tutter
Will not be your kryptonite.
Although you may talk faster
than a speeding locomotive…
They instilled the mentality
I could leap mountains
With a single thought.

I was raised in a house full of women
Where I was walking distance
To grade school
But I still got escorted onto school grounds.
My guards ready to sacrifice
Their lives at a moment's notice
If a stray bullet ever found its way in my
vicinity.
Both Secret Service and First Ladies.
Our dinner table was the Oval Office.
Where executive decisions were made.

We watched Oprah Winfrey at 4pm every day.
Oprah, more than a woman in our home
Oprah, more than a rape survivor
Oprah, more than a survivor of domestic violence
Oprah, more than someone fired in her 20s
living in her car

Oprah was the living embodiment of
Black girl magic
Before the phrase was ever coined.

I was raised in a house full of women.
Who served first and ate last.
Who worked hard and
Prayed on knees even harder.
Where I learned the true meaning of
Restorative justice and
Martial law.
Where I saw the gospel
Every day of the week
Not just Sunday in service.
Where posters of Jerry Rice and Joe Montana
hung off walls like banners.
But I,
The biggest sports fan
Was not allowed to set a foot on the
football field.
So I made out from behind the bleachers.

I was raised in a house full of women.
Where wooden cabinets
Held more secrets than Tupperware.
If you dusted for prints,
You'd find that no matter
How organized those shelves were,
Family matters were messy.
Where my grandmother
Was victim to the hands of violence
Risking her life for children
Who were told they're not worth shit.

Who were lined up on Friday nights and
Brainwashed into thinking that nobody
Would pay a nickel for them.
My grandfather who never
Hurt a single hair on my head was a veteran.
Like his father before him.
Like my father.
And uncle.
And cousin.
I come from a long line of men
Who serve our country
And leave their honor on the battlefield.
No wonder I've had a hard time my whole life
Trusting a man or following authority.

I was raised in a house full of women
Who were the ones
With Purple Hearts.
I stood down to their command.
Today I stand up for their rights,
I salute them for every sacrifice
I never knew about.
But I knew they put
Food on the table,
Compassion in my broken heart,
And young boy that had no business
Making it past 18,
Through a 4 year university.

I was raised in a house full of
beautiful Black women
Where I learned to embrace

My masculine and
I learned to embrace my feminine
But I choose to lead with the latter.
Where fellowship was the only thing
That ever kept me out of the
footsteps of my father.
Away from the rival gangs.
Arm's distance from excuses.
And a whole galaxy away from
The myth
That
WOMEN
Need a
Man
To
SURVIVE.

Head full of kinks

My mother calls me at the airport.
Wants to know the last time
I washed my hair.
Curious if I know anybody in
Denver, Colorado who can
do me a favor and braid IT.
Says hair should not look like this
In the public.

Nappy.
Head full of kinks.

Says I did not raise you to look like that.
Says Jeremy,
It'll be a goddamn shame if your hair twist up.
Little does she know
She's already committed blasphemy.
Jesus Christ had dreads and I'm planning on
growing some.
She solicits $20 from her wallet to let
Her comb it out.

I tell her
Mother,
I have never met a comb strong enough
That can walk a mile in my afro.
That it has broken more rows of teeth
Than Cassius Clay in his prime.
That I've had to retire
More rat tails than thoroughbreds.

That I've had to float past negative comments
my whole life like a butterfly.
And this Jamaican castor oil mixed with
shea butter
have created a recipe
So sweet that bees land on my head and
mistake me for a flower.

I have enough pollen, melanin and stardust
to create
my own ecosystem.
And if I can withstand 32 trips
around the Sun
then I'll survive one more conversation
with my mother
under a microscope.

My mother doesn't understand me.
She's never taken the time to understand me.

She doesn't understand my tangled hair is a
metaphor for this country
And if I straighten it,
It'll lose its native roots.
Besides,
My dignity is not for sale.

Andrew Jackson
Who sits on that very bill
Will not have any more stock
In the ownership of Black bodies.
He owned 150 enslaved people
In his lifetime.

And while I am no slave to money
He will not have the pleasure of
Profiting in death.
He can roll in his grave before I ever
forfeit one of my coils
For cash.
He once placed an ad
In the Tennessee Gazette,
Looking for a 5'10" Mulatto man slave.
Promising a $50 reward for his capture
And $10 extra for every 100 lashes
that he took.

While my mother
Rich with good intentions
Has robbed me of my self-esteem.
Has overdrawn from an account
She has never contributed to.
Her first born, ME,
Has given her more second chances
Than anybody else in my life I know.
She likes to remind me:
Jeremy, I am your mother.
I brought you into this world.
And I am too broken and too ashamed
to admit how many times
I've tried to take myself out of it.

There are too many days of the week
That I wake up and
I do not take pride in my Blackness.
I look in the mirror.
See Loch Ness.
See Chupacabra.

See Godzilla.
God only knows,
It's taken most my life to actually like what's
in the reflection
But it takes my mother a few words to set off
explosives.
She doesn't understand the topic of hair
In my culture is a land mine.
She says I blow everything out of proportion
But I am more ticking time bomb
Than actual person.

The days of the week that I wake up
And do my hair,
I get mistaken for Polynesian.
At least they acknowledge me on
the bus.
When I'm lazy
And throw it in a beanie,
they treat me like a Muslim
Until they hear the bass
In my voice
And if you
Listen up close,
You might even catch the Blues.
But when I dance,
That rhythm
is synonymous
With being African American.
To be Black is to feel invisible
In my natural state
Yet celebrated
Whenever I assimilate.
Trauma manifests itself

In bodies just like this.
My mother says I am so handsome
When I clean up.
But I have cleaned out
Images with a 5 o'clock shadow
and my deep waves.
My mother is still living in the past.
Which is why she wants me to
Set my clock back
Back to before that disease came
And took out all my curls.
And everything came back
More wooly than curly.

And while I am
Just 30 something
I'm not sure every time my mother
Looks at me if
She sees my father or her baby.
Either way we've both abandoned her.

*I wish loving a Black man on no one
in this country.
I wish loving a Black man on no one
in this world.*

I'm at the baggage claim
A double entendre
My bag
The last one left.
My mother asks to FaceTime me.
I decline.
I know she would not like what she saw
On the other line.

And I love my mother far too much,
More than anything.
And I would hate
To disappoint her
this many times
in one full day.

On the rocks

My stepfather
Sends me an email
On the night of
My 32nd birthday.

Tells me he listened to a YouTube clip
When I spoke on the subject
Of toxic masculinity
As a special guest on a podcast in LA.

I should have guessed
A while ago that any day now,
He would resurface again.

Tells me to give
Him a call.
That there is
No time like the present
To reconnect.
But there was a time
He called me a sociopath,
On MySpace.

We never addressed
How I manipulate
My poetry into burlesque.
Stripping down to the core
Is a quality
That comes
With lots of

Friend requests.
He is not the first
On a grocery list of men
Who have hurt me
And wiped their
Hands clean.
Who have
Walked away
And then reappeared.
Cuckoos are known
To trick
Other birds
Into raising
Their youngsters.

I come from a generation
Where we thank the women
Who raised us.

That don't fly with me.

See
I have learned
How dangerous it is
To fall in love with potential.
How men in our
Culture can
Potentially leave you
at the altar.

It's hard to groom Black boys.
How many of your favorite emcees
That wanna be basketball players
Or vise versa

Say the real MVP is their mothers?
My stepfather
Taught me how
To dribble a ball
Then bounced like
A free-agent.
Has the audacity to
Tell me not to run
When I've seen him do suicide drills
For a living.
In the last decade
He must of acquired enough
Speed, endurance and agility
To become a Harlem Globetrotter.
Meanwhile I am guilt-tripped
If I pass up on the
Long distance alley-oop.

Excuse me if I hardly desire
To call time-out
Of my schedule.

Says he can offer some insight.
And while I know he's got game
I think he's out of boundaries.

He says
I am doing a great disservice
By placing our talk on the back burner.
He doesn't know
How often I've done cocaine off the glass,
And over time
I've failed at everything but suicide.
I've had to rebound from every addiction.

The greatest disservice that could ever be done
now is the pot calling the kettle black.

I wanted to press criminal charges on him
The day he hijacked my mother's smile.
Wanted to drive cross country to Houston
The weekend I got my driver's license
And premeditate a hit and run.

But now.
I just wanna take it slow.
I think we should both take it slow.
I reply to his email a week later.
Cause I'm on colored people time.
But that's another story.
And whether my prescription contacts were dry
Or my Pandora Station decided to play
Luther Vandross,
Dance With My Father,
Either way, that night
My eyes were in heavy precipitation.

My relationships with older Black men
Like my scotch,
Tend to be on the rocks.
But I am a skilled sailor.
Even better with the rock
In my hands.
It might be too late
To lace up my Nikes,
And play my stepfather
In a game of horse.
But it is never too late
To forgive.

Skeletons in my closet

I remember
The first time
My high school coach called a teammate a
Pussy
I laughed.
Howling
Like wolves we hurled
That 5 letter word
Like a shot put.
We got the biggest kick outta
Subjecting a young man
To the degradation of
A female reproductive organ.
That talk ran all the way
From the track field
Back to the locker room.

It was such a laughing matter
That sometimes
We even threw mud on his
Name when we hit the showers.
It's only funny until someone
Gets hurt.
Then it's hilarious.
I don't know if he
Went home and iced his wounds
With a bag of
"boys will be boys"
Or took epsom salt baths
To reduce the pain of mobbing.

I'm not sure if there
Was a member
In his household
He was able to talk to
But around coach
He always appeared
To be treading on thin ice.
I don't know
What he did
In his free time
To tend to his ego
But whenever I saw him
Walking around
By himself at lunch
And said hi
I'm sure it was the
Equivalent of
Spitting in his face.

I wonder if any of
The voices he had in his head
Ever told him to
Call a help hotline.
But I know
He was the scapegoat
For a bunch
Of Douchebags
Who wanted
To be liked
More than we
Wanted to do
The right thing.

Us
A pack of
Bystanders trying
To manage our
Raging testosterone
Were too busy
Trying to be in the
Good graces
Of a man
Going through a
Mid life crisis
Who suffered
From Napoleon Complex.

Us
Posing like men
Were too scared to jump
In the line of Fire
So we used
Our teammate
As a punch line.

But when our
Teammate committed
Suicide
It wasn't a joke.

I high jumped
Every question
I was asked
About his well-being.
Coach said he
Lacked mental toughness.
We said nothing.

Our silence, betrayal enough.
We hurdled over the dark cloud
He left behind in his wake.

I woke up too many days in
My junior year with night terrors.
Tardy to school
Because of the guilt trips I went on
before first period.
The only senior superlative award
I should have won was
Most likely to watch someone
hang themselves
and sprint in the
opposite direction.
It was clear
The demons my teammate
Was trying to outrun
He couldn't get away from
And although he was a
Damn good distance runner
It was his teammates that
Were his Achilles heel.

We
The shin splints
Did not give him the
Rest he needed to heal
Instead we
Called him too sensitive
Insisted our words were
no Big Deal.
When in fact
We took turns

In the 4x100
Meter relay race
Of running him
Straight into the Grave.

If one of us
Had the fortitude
To drop the baton
Much to the dismay
Of our coach
Our teammate
Would be here with us
Instead of serving as another
Name on a long list of
Skeletons we keep in our closet.

War Stories

Founder's day of my fraternity
Passed
And not a member of my chapter
Reached out to me.
If it wasn't for the
Broken family
I came from
I probably wouldn't of joined
In the first place.

The last time I
Spoke out about
Someone who died
Pledging
I got death threats.
I received the cold shoulder years ago.
Isolation is nothing new to me.
The effects
Of groupthink
Still ripple
Into adulting.

Used to tell
My students to
Pledge a
Black Fraternity
Until I realized
The nightmares
From undergrad
Still accompany me.

As a grown-up
I have tried to
Make amends
For the atrocities
I have committed
With these
Very hands that
Pour into the same
People I once stripped
Of their humanity.
That's partly why
Demonic movies don't move me
But the horror I've committed
On Black boys seeking
Brotherhood in my past life
Still haunts me.

I'll never shake the image
Of that freshman
I gave a seizure to.
A tear just left my eye
As I reminisce
But it's weightless
In comparison
To what he'll tell his kids
When they say
They wanna stomp the yard.

I got scars
On my body
That give confessions
I never had the
Courage to speak on
But there's far deeper wounds

That I still cover
With the paraphernalia
I put on.
I skipped the fine print
When I was seeking
Membership.
The things I've done
To belong
Make me
Ashamed most times
They cross my mind
But

Hazing teaches you
How to be more
Wallpaper than love story.
Gift wrap the ugly truth.
Put a bow on it.
Choose the color.
Crimson and cream
Royal blue and white
Purple and gold
Brown and yellow
But beneath
All the tissue paper
Is the scar tissue we neglect.

You see boys
So desperate of a
Ceremonial middle passage
They'll jeopardize freedom.
I see members
Who got branded
And I can't help but think

How thirsty for validation
We are
That we'll throw ourselves
Into the fire just to show
The world it cannot
Burn us

That we are birthed from
The inferno
Even if the flame casts
A shadow that will
Follow us until we disintegrate.

So prepared
At wits' end
They'll do anything
To cross the burning sand
Even if they gotta reenact
The brutality of
Ancestors' firsthand.

Such as stuffing
Ourselves into compromising situations
Like forefathers were in slave ships.
I know lawyers
Who'd get the book
Thrown at them
If Snapchat was around
During our intake.
I'll never forget the look
On my grandmother's face
When she asked me to
Pull my pants down.
Hate to admit that I still own

That same paddle
That caused internal
Bleeding in my storage unit.

I know lots of broken men
Walking around willing to die to
Join the same organization
That stole a part of me
I'll never reclaim.
I can never take back
The words I used to
Demean another brotha
Who probably was on
An academic scholarship.
His mother who
Sent him
To the one place
She thought he'd be safe.

I stopped going to
Coming out shows because I'm
Over the masquerade.
Don't wanna shuck & jive
In a Letterman jacket
At a probate or a party
When it'd be more appropriate
To parade in a burial shroud.
Too many of us trying to be OWT
In Greek attire
When we should be strolling
In a prison jumpsuit.

I know that by even
Sharing this

I've already committed
Treason.
But we have went so far off road
From the vision of the founders,
I can no longer
Stomach the mission statement.
Unlike our armed services
We don't receive $3,000
A month for the
The combat fatigue
Or shell shock
We put each other through
But one day
I hope my line brothers
And I can get together
And talk about something
Without
Trading war stories.

Holding Cell

The first time I was incarcerated
I cried myself to sleep.
My grandmother
lying on her deathbed
needed me to assist
with her dialysis treatment
But instead of helping her
with her kidney failure
I was too busy filling mine
with guilty pleasures.

Treating myself to
two meals in correctional facilities.
I wish I could of nursed
her to back to life
But her loss of appetite
was directly proportionate
to my appetite for destruction.

There's a type
of hopelessness that comes
with being a caregiver
and my lack of faith
combined with my
toxic self-loathing
made me a glutton
for punishment.
I became desensitized.

Every mugshot

at some point
felt increasingly more
like yearbook photos
than police records.
I learned how to
master bowel movements
in front of outsiders
while simultaneously
flushing my four years of higher education
down the drain.

Down in the dumps
I could've created a noose
from my deepest despair.
Guards felt more like slave catchers
than fellow human beings.
I began to believe every word
they called me.
I forgot how to answer
to my own name.
I became

Another number.
Another statistic.
Another jail bird.

Each wing stop
looking in the
rear view
my glory days
seemed further
behind.
Between each
holding cell

I found more comfort knowing
I accomplished more
than I was ever expected to.
That I could only
outrun the inevitable
until I got a charley horse.
That my story
was more tragedy
than fairytale.

I came to the conclusion
that I was going to lose the person
in the world that knew me best so
during this free fall I corroborated
with everything I'd ever been told as a juvenile
but as all the naysaying came into fruition
I reaped nothing but rotten luck.

As a prodigal son
that didn't fall far.
It became easier to
blame my father
for the path he paved
But with every acre of asphalt
I now carefully laid
What I didn't forgive I
eventually became.

My grandmother
was scheduled to have
her foot removed during
one of my stints locked up.
I'd rather of lost my ability to permanently speak
than expect the person on her last breath

to use her final retirement check
to fund bail for my latest mistake.

My aunt told me after
I came home
When she found out I was back again
she asked Nana for help and she replied:
We have to get him out.
We're all he has.

She should have left me where I was
but she was right
I had nobody.

In the midst of my
self-disintegration
I could barely
protect myself.
With every reflection that
became more unfamiliar to me
I was losing the ability to
recognize myself
But the
love in the air
was thicker
than the smoke.

She passed away
when I was awaiting trial.
I left a trail of tears
thinking I was a medicine cabinet
to someone who tried
everything they could
to help me get

back on my two feet
when they were
barely able to stand on one.

I keep a Trinidadian flag
on my nightstand.
My grandma visits
me in my dreams
her health renewed.
She was there
when I fell from glory.
My road to redemption
was not as easy to pave as my destruction.
Not as innocent like the
building blocks I played
with as an infant.
But each baby step
reminded me
no matter how frequently
I fell I was gaining footing.

Whenever I march
into a juvenile hall
to give a motivational word
I am confident before I speak
that nobody is beyond saving.
This is why I go the distance
to advocate because I know
the dugouts better than
I know the nosebleeds
because it
used to be home base for me.

I go to bat for those caught in the
school-to-prison pipeline.
And like the bases loaded in
the World Series
I aim for McCovey Cove.

*I CAME TO DISRUPT HOPELESSNESS
BECAUSE I HAD IT DONE FOR ME.*

Twelfth Step

I visited a rehab center yesterday.
A few short years removed
From the seats
I Occupied.
I, a recovering addict, knew
Depression like my next-door neighbor
Who came over uninvited.
Walked in like they had a spare.

But as the key-note today,
I think I saw
The next Picasso.
He bled watercolors
from his fingertips
Like he was holding
A shard of glass.
In a room full
Of shattered hope
His veins pumped
Enough acrylic paint
To transform
All the sunken eyes
Into rainbows.

'Cause heaven knows
They've been a shadow
Of themselves for
Longer than they'd like to admit.
And for them to walk outta
This room with a smile

Or a ray of hope
Would be a meteorological
Phenomenon of its own.

But that would require me
To be a reflection
Of light in water
And since the
General consensus
Of anguish before me
is deep as
Oceans
I am both mirror and window.

Myself...like my art
Is a work in progress.
That doesn't stop
Me from reminding them
That Rome was built
On ruins
And what more fitting
Of an analogy is it
To be human.

Human error is
How I even got here.
My father and mother
Were both the black sheep
Of their family
Yet together
They created a masterpiece.

I saw a philosopher
Take his power back

Against his withdrawals.
Tiny glimpses of Aristotle
Cuts in his arm
More like papyrus scrolls.
Music and poetry rolled
Off his tongue like
The enchanting flow of
Trevi Fountain
Beautifying this
Indoor space.
Those around him
Dehydrated.
Getting a momentary splash
Whether they wanted it
Or not.
He was a symphony
Of great ideas and
Bad decisions.
I saw shakiness
In between syllables
But could only
Imagine the racing thoughts.
Today, his engine light flashed
With every confession.
This smog check was
Long overdue.
During this mass group therapy
We rolled out
Of our comfort zone.

Now auto-bots
No longer seeking
Refuge in a junkyard.
I did not need

A metal detector
To find the most overlooked
Treasure in the city
Buried alive.

These were not
Damaged goods.
They were diamonds
In the rough.
I had no idea
What I was looking for
When I woke
Up that morning
But what I found was
Fragments of my father
In every survivor.

See
There is an art
In broken things.
In Japan it's called
Kintsugi.
The method of
Recognizing the beauty
In broken objects.
Restoring them with lacquer
Instead of throwing them away
By the wayside.

We should practice that with humans.

I saw my brother today
In that rehab center.
6 degrees of separation

Between us.
I pierced the eyes
Of a stranger and recognized myself
When he said he's been called
A mutt his whole life.
My ears went up like a dog
At the sound of his pain
And in his delivery
I heard Tupac but
He was the
Provocative evidence
That the hate you give
Little infants
Hurts everyone.

I have a passport
In my pocket that I
Haven't used all year
But a couple moments
In this space
Was like taking a trip
To a foreign land.
And I tell my newly
Gathered journeymen
That when men
Come together in a
Brave space like this
The world heals.
But part of the prerequisite
Of being a prophet
Requires suffering.

Upon exit I provide
The book I wrote
This time two years prior
So they can get
High off this supplier.
One of them grabs me
On his way out
To his road to recovery
And says
Thanks
for the Ted Talk.

Beautiful Chaos

I am no morning person
But lately
Her words
Have been
The perfect
Pick-me-up.
I like waking up
To the aroma of
Fresh thoughts.
She is more
Garden than
Snack.
The way she cultivates
Chrysanthemums
From imperfect
And broken
Is the thumbprint
Of an alchemist.

Her piece of mind
a delicacy.
And with every literary device
I receive another serving.
How I love to see
Her wits brewing.
Her inner bruja
In tune
With the earth
And her gifts.
In each limerick

You can hear
Her hostage voice
Escaping the wreckage.
Relocating to a place
Where only blind men see
Through the lines
Of her haiku.

Each syllable cutting to
The point.
Cutting deep enough
To slit wrists open.
Severing ties from
Users and abusers
That made her believe
A eulogy was
The best thing
That would ever
Come from her.
But if you
Read her sonnets
You'd think
An assembly line
Of beautiful chaos
Would best describe her.

How my eyes
Dampen at the construction
Of her imagery.
How she's
Spent most her life
Folded up like origami
Surrounded by toxic waste
But still

She grew wings.
You can expect
Flashes of brilliance
During every brainstorm.
I know she's experienced
The kinds of lows
Few live to tell
Survived the kind of childhood
that would kill a Gladiator.
Are you not entertained?
But hailing
From parts unknown
She's weathered
Every tempest.
And at her
Highest latitude
She glimmers
Like the Northern Lights.
I know there is no place I'd rather be
Than in the waves
Being pulled
Into her tide.

I can be
Literal.
I can be
Abstract.
I can be
Myself.
I see in
Living color.
Tone deaf
To shades of grey.

I can
See the riot
In between the
Margins.
I picket
With my ball point.
She said my
Passion penetrates deeply
Into areas she wasn't sure existed.
And since she
Is already against
The grain,
I go
3 wheel drive
Off-roading.
Turning this
Stationary paper
Into a writer's block.
Let the street lights
Serve as a high beam
As we cross the interstate.

Our chakras are aligned.
I like rhythm with her
In all of its forms.
Momentarily
The earth doesn't
Seem so round.
I'm flat footed
Until I feel
That Love Jones.
Then I'm the
Blues in your
Left thigh,

Trying to be the
The funk
In your right.

I tend to
Come alive
In the nighttime,
But as of late,
Her words
Have been the
Perfect lullaby.
I like sleeping
To the fragrance
Of burned incense.
Oh how she has lit something in me.

She is more
Nightcap than
Midnight munchies.
Not jumping to conclusions
But she has
Become such
Music
To my soul.
Countless ensembles.
I am not preaching
To the choir.
I am singing in it.
How sweet the sound.
She is the poetry
I have yet to write.

My first language

Lorna,
Do you know
You cross my mind so often
I'm beginning
To think I
Get my jaywalking from you.
I Hate to curb
Your enthusiasm
But there
Are days
I'd wish to be
Be hit by
Oncoming traffic
Instead of
Continuing this
Ongoing fight for
Freedom.
But
I'm really happy you
Migrated here
From the
West Indies
When you did.
Times are different now.

You would be
Completely criminalized
Because you wanted
Better lives for your children
When your only

Crime was never
Putting yourself first.
Although you were
Second to none
Whether you received
Salt from your husband
Or pepper spray
From the border
It seems you were born
To be a condiment.
Condemned to be
Indentured servants or
Objects of affection.
Women
In our culture
Have always lived
In debt to someone else.

Your skin
More sandpaper
Than melanin
Did not splinter
From insults.
How you made
Silk from slander
Was a work of heart
I think I tailored after.
And despite
Stereotypes
You did more than
Pop out babies
And hide
stretch marks.
You could thread the needle.

Grandma.
You loved me
As a seamstress.
Stitching
The pages of
My broken heart.
My first language
Was love
because of you.

So I am more
Open book than
Slave to my thoughts.
I must be
Kin of Nat Turner.
You came
Into this world
Just before
We were considered
Royalty.
Although my teachers
Said we were
Property.
I'd like
To think we were
Always
More cream of
The crop than
Chitlins.
I know
You never came
From a "shithole country."

I wish
I asked you
More questions.
Like why
Didn't you choose
Canada?
What captivated you
About
The American Dream
And did you work
Graveyard shifts
Because
You found
That it was out of reach
Or because
You'd Rest In Peace
If one of us could
Grasp it with a
Decent education?

I have sown my
Wild oats
Many times over
Since your absence.
It used to be hard
During the holidays
But I don't drink
Nearly as much.
Some days
I don't like it here.
So I complain.
I am told
To go back
To Africa

And although
It is a compliment,
It is a luxury
I do not have.
I know immigrants
That work seven days
A week.
Who clean
Houses for a living
Then go back "home"
Too weak to
Play with
Their own kids.
I wonder if they
Ever consider
Going back home
On vacation?
Just so they can
Speak their
First language.

'Cause here
Thick accents
Can get you
Treated like
A second rate citizen.
Looking
Un-American can
Get you detained.
I know why
The caged bird sings.

Nana.
You must of risen up

Like condors
Bald eagles
When you were denied
entrance into restaurants.
Did you ever go into denial
When they didn't
Serve your kind?
How did
Kindness
Remain
Your first language?
I'm trying
To leave
Your granddaughter
As the heir
To our throne
With all the dirt
America gave
Us in our face.
How you took that dirt
Grew gardens
Fed entire communities
I'll never know.

Excuses never
Proliferated off your lips.
You hit the ground running
I shoulda known
You'd raise some road
Runners.
But our people don't
Slow dance nearly
enough.
Look how

Fast we got here.
Currently there are
nearly 70,000
Immigrant children
In the custody
Of the United States.

Abuela.
Over 20,000 people
Raised 13 million dollars
In 4 days
To build a wall.
Not to feed our hungry.
Or to provide clean water.
Or to clothe and house innocents,
But for the erection of an idol
Fashioned by their fear.

You used to sing
"Child, things
Are gonna get easier."
Did you mean
When we reunite?
Or in another century?
Or was there an
Underlying message?
I listen to Childish Gambino
And can't help but think

This is America.

How the hood loves us

I keep a
Backwood wrapper
Tucked in the verse
Of my favorite scripture.
I do not smoke
Religiously
But with a 1/2 glass of red wine after a
Full day of being Black in America
It's quite the blessing.

I haven't had indica in
Three weeks.
But let me be blunt
You can't walk
Down my neighborhood
Without seeing an eighth grader with a
Pre-roll tucked behind his eardrum.

Ran into one of my former students
At Philz coffee shop.
Told me he was happy
That he could hug me on school days
Harder than he could the block.
Dropped an eighth of weed
Off in my hand and disappeared.
But this the city where
We pass joints
Not judgment.

Did I tell you how the hood loves us?

In love with us
But not enough to
Let us live.
A week later he was killed in a
Drive-by.
He used to tell me:
"Jeremy, the city will read
about me. They will know my name."
He was right.

He made the Obituary.

His mother asked me to speak at his funeral.
It was loud.
But all the endo
Couldn't drown out
The suffering we all felt though.
She said I turned his life around.
I wish I could of turned back the hands of time
to when I first saw him
Finishing off a roach.
And invited him to Bible study
But I didn't wanna bug him.

I log into Instagram.
I see his homies on the corner
Of 3rd and Palou.
Chilling off that sativa.
Drinking a fifth of whiskey.
Wearing a XXL in memory shirt
Firearm tucked under their New Religion jeans.

Did I tell you how the hood loves us?

His son not even
Potty trained
Has to grow up in the same
District where the killers caught
His pops slipping at.
Streets is watching
But a lot can get past you
When you cross-faded.
It doesn't help that
City officials
Turn a blind eye.
But no rest for the weary,
Within 3 weeks
There's a graffiti piece
In his honor.

I love murals
Because they're a form
Of three-dimensional storytelling
But I hate them because
I wish we could reshuffle the deck
And change the cards so our kids
Can live long enough to kiss
They children on the collarbones
Instead of becoming
An artistic reminder that

This is how the hood loves us.

Maybe God has bigger plans
For us in His kingdom
Than He does for us right here.
Maybe God needs a pair

Of strong arms
And a sturdy back.
Maybe God depends on
Our liveliness
More than our families
Yearn for our longevity.
Maybe we're building a treehouse
In heaven because we don't see those
In the hood.
We see more dispensaries
Than libraries.
Surprised we haven't
broken into the libraries
Taken the books,
Ripped out the pages,
And used them for rolling papers.
Trapped in this food desert it makes
Perfect sense
Why my community is surrounded by
Gun shops and
Liquor stores.

But if you take MUNI
Down to AT&T Park
You'll get the finest lobster tail
This side of the Pacific.
But I heard in the hood
The McRib is back for a limited time.

This is how the hood loves us.

I voted for my first Black mayor
Last Spring.

She said she'll Golden Gate Bridge
The opportunity gap.
She ran off the backing of the perfect
Hybrid
Retired pimps
Turned non-profit gurus
And former gang members
Now
Self-made entrepreneurs.
She promised little boys and girls
She'd give her all to
Reshaping our neighborhoods.
But I guess when the dust was settled
Some of the smoke clouded her memory.

This is how the hood loves us.

She said she was a different type of Breed.
She hired hundreds of new police officers
In the first week to
Clean up the streets.
Maybe they'll help us
Dab into a new pair of handcuffs.
Or catch us hopping BART
Cause it's too expensive
And instead of the
Youth riding for free
Teach them how to play dead.
But even while we're alive
You gotta ask yourself
What kind of quality of life is this?

Inequity looks like our children
Living with Type I Diabetes

Before they even
Get looked at by
A division one team.
How is Tyrone gonna make
Varsity team armless?
I guess a strain of
Gorilla Glue
Might hold him together for a bit.

The only thing sweet
About living in the city
Is the swishers.

Because this is how the hood loves us.

Who will survive in America

I'm on My Way Home
listening to the Late Registration.
I wanted some black music,
That real Crack Music,
Everyone has their Addiction.
And when I'm the designated driver
Mine is Def Jam recordings.
I took my fingers off the wheel,
To see if I had enough strength,
To make a Diamond with my bare hands.

I still got it...
Like I was back in my dormitory days,
When nothing could
Bring Me Down,
Before my student loans turned into
The debt I owe that can
Touch the Sky.
But tonight...
I Heard 'Em Say
The road was slippery
On account of the thick fog.
Ya never know,
So I forsake the carpool lane
And use low beams on the back roads,
trying to Drive Slow,
the Street Lights my only company.
Pumping my brakes,
The subwoofer sounds

Like it had Rolling Stones,
Best album of 2005 in full spin
Rattling in the trunk.
My grandfather in the front seat,
With me listening to Roses,
Which is ironic 'cause he's as
Illinois as they come.

Used to be a Monster of the Midway,
But has bloomed like a daylily
In his elder days.
Evidence that some of us need
More time to reach
Our wonder years.
My daughter asleep in the back,
Been gone since we passed the grapevine.
Tired out from the Celebration,
She boarded her first plane.
Rode window seat on Southwest.
Tonight she counts sheep,
Under the North Star.
Homey, We Major.
It's Late,
And right before I pull into
The assigned parking spot,
The last song that plays is Hey Mama.
And I can't help but think
If Kim is encouraging Ye
To go back to school.
Or is he too busy
Keeping up with the Kardashians?

I was one of the many
That the College Dropout

Kept in school but
Ever since he got kidnapped by
The Klan,
His Blood On The Leaves
I want to scream WAKE UP MR. WEST,
I See You in My Nightmares,
But he's been stuck in a sunken place
for so long,
I don't know if he would hear me.

If he could GET OUT his own way
He'd probably have a star on
Hollywood's Walk of Fame.
But these days on-air meltdowns have
Become his most famous single.
The topic of mental health
A broken record.
But part of me thinks
He never recovered
From 808 & Heartbreak.

There was a time in the prime
I would of sacrificed a kidney
To be floor level
For his Glow in the Dark tour.
Or I'd talk off someone's ear
In defense that he was
A top 5 emcee.
Who knew I'd Van Gogh him.

When I took him out of my playlist,
It was like I lost two people.
The Champion and the music.
I never saw the day

That he would die a hero,
But I hate that he lived long enough
To become the villain.
The day he marched his
Air Yeezys into the White House,
To grovel at the feet of a president,
Who uses our people as a footrest.
That was the day he no longer
Walked on water.

He said murder rates
Have been down 20%
Every year in Chi-Raq.
He must of been referring
To his album sales.
Maybe it's all the Flashing Lights
that got him confused,
but 72 people were shot
In the Windy City
A year prior
Waiting on that Good Life.

When he put on the MAGA hat,
Said he felt like Superman,
I wanted to hang up my cape,
Like Henry Cavill.
And this is why
We are warned
Not to worship false Gods.
Also, I don't know
If we read the same comic.
I doubt the symbol of hope
Would co-sign
The bane of our existence.

I don't know if the person
Who immigrated from planet Krypton
Would play the same hand in
Pelting refugees with tear gas.
Super breath does not look like
Giving voice
to the new Jim Crow laws.
My idea of X-ray vision
Does not include
Viewing any race capable
Of infesting a country.

Because the dehumanization of a people
Is how ethnic cleansing begins.

Kanye.
Did you learn anything
From Auschwitz?
Through the Wire
Was a classic but
Jews really were surrounded
By double-barbed,
Electrical fences.

But the more you spaz out,
I'm not sure if it's because you're missing
Your meds or your mother.
She was a professor.
She was 1 of the best.
But 6 million Jews died.
Show us her Mercy.

Over 11 million lives were wiped out
By a man who used fear as the fuel

To drive a nail
Right down a nation.
And if I can be Frank
It's happening again.

Ever since you said slavery was a choice,
I'm beginning to think
The doctors should've kept your mouth wired
shut, Kanye.
How could you be so Heartless?
Your name in Yoruba means
"Next in line to the chieftaincy."
I was first in line with my Big Brother,
Paying with nickels and dimes
To pick up Graduation,
When 50 Cent vowed he would retire if
You outsold him.
I lined up to Watch the Throne
With other brothers and sisters,
When it looked like you were next in line
To inherit Roc-A-Fella,
Ready to bring balance to Hip Hop.

But you switched sides like a cassette.
We should of seen Anakin in your future,
But the anarchy in your message,
Gave us a New Hope.
I'm hoping your beautiful,
Dark, twisted fantasy
Is far from over.

Jesus is King
but you are not.
And as for my people

We will figure out
Who Will Survive in America
Who Will Survive in America
Who Will Survive in America
Who Will Survive in America
When it All Falls Down.

People ignited

A Mexican walks into a bar
Requests a Corona
After a long day of hard work

Before the glass
Can touch his drink coaster,
A local patron asks him for his papers.

His driver's license
Not enough proof
He is a legal citizen.
His blue collar
Doesn't work here.

Besides
For him to earn
A seat at this table
He had to
Steal a job from
Someone else

Caucasian investigation ensues
Expecting proof of insurance.
This is a routine traffic stop.
Red light
That could lead to yellow tape
If he pulls out a green card.

This Mexican forgets he
Has to come to grip
With the fact

He is the elephant in every room now.

We must have skin tough
As armadillo,
But no matter how many times
We are called animals,

We do not curl up into a ball.

He has to swallow the bitter pill
That a clown, disguised in sheep's clothing,
Sits in the most powerful chair in his country.

Who at any minute
Could start a nuclear war
With the touch of a button.

But at the moment
#45's fingers are pointed at someone else,
Like an silver-spooned infant
Who came from privilege
And now does everything
He can to hold onto power,
Or grew up viewing everyone
Else as 'other'
And as an adult struggles to play nicely with
others.

Those fingers...probably were occupied sending
off a 280 character tweet,
That is laced in lies
Or reeks of cyber-bullying.
With his hand
Constantly fondling women,
Because when you have money

They let you grab them by the pussy,
Without consent.

But in a crooked world you can afford to
Pay off lawyers
After shaming victims
And victimizing yourself.

Put millions into the palm
Of an attorney
In the form of hush money
And non-disclosure agreements.
And appoint rapists and drunks
To the Supreme Court to
Hand out justice…

All while his wife,
Leads an 'anti-bullying campaign.'
When she's not busy
Plagiarizing the words of Black women,
She is visiting brown children
In detention centers,
The same center that a Fox news anchor
Likened to summer camps.
There are 70,000 still in the custody
Of private prisons.

I wonder if they're still playing
Water game Olympics in the Winter time.
Or how many dozens of antidepressants were
Forced into mouths of minors before their
Tabletop game tournaments.
Or how many pages of handwritten
Letters they've scrapbooked for their parents

Since they last appeared in deportation court
alone as a toddler.
The devil doesn't always wear Prada.
Sometimes they wear
Trench coats but
'I really don't care, do you?'

With her husband,
And his toupee that flies off the rail
Nearly as much as him
Whenever a journalist so much as
Fixes their mouth to ask him
A real question.

Approval ratings low like
The chances I have of walking down
The street in broad daylight and 911 not being
Dialed on me for merely 'breathing.'
I could be shot
In my grandmother's backyard.
Or in my own apartment so...

I'm not afraid of walking into
The wrong neighborhood anymore
When cops are the ones doing all the drive-bys.

It's been a few weeks
Since I last heard somebody speak
Spanish out loud.
Afraid the next time
Their native tongue
Sings like a caged bird,
ICE agents might plunge into them
Headfirst like pelicans,

Pulling them out of the water like salmon
Disrupting the school of fish.
Uprooting them because our
Government branch has been
Hi-jacked by a Klansman.
This same Klansman
Who thinks it's smart
To brand teachers with guns
To prevent school shootings.
Like almost 300 mass shooting this year wasn't
enough.

Back to school shopping is already a challenge.
It's hard enough to find jeans that fit my
Daughter at Old Navy because of her height.
It will be a tall order
To find a bullet-proof backpack.

This same Klansman-in-chief
Shoots himself in the foot every time he speaks.
He has emboldened racists
To crawl from under their rocks.
Too worried about people with pigment
and how they will 'infest' America
Has encouraged wolves in
Make America Great Again hats

To huff,
And puff,
And blow down

Every. Single. Right.
That we, the people,
Can peacefully assemble

Without feeling
Like we are in an episode of the Twilight Zone.

This feels more like the final season
Of The Apprentice
Than it does the home of the brave.
We are Left
standing in a house of cards.

I wore a breathing mask for 2 weeks straight
Because of the most destructive fire
In California's history
But I should have known
Settlers do not know how to steward the land.
He blamed it on poor forest management.
I wish when he came to visit the ashes,
He was lost in them.

Peculiar,
The smoke has dissipated but America is
still in flames,
its people IGNITED.
Those who feel they are without sin,
Because they read their bible,
Tithe at church
Have a confederate flag
Hanging off their Dodge 4-by-4,
And watch football religiously.

They
Are casting stones,
In every direction.
Meanwhile,
I am on my knees every night

Pondering if we both pray
To the same God.

I don't have the answers.
But I do know a Corona with lime
Cancels out the bitterness
And since we are living in bittersweet times,
I go to the bar to get one.

It seems too appropriate.
And legend has it,
The first wedge of lime
Put into a bottle of Mexican beer stuck there.
Literally and permanently.

Just like us.

At the border

And if you give even a cup of cold water,
To one of these little ones who is my disciple,
you will surely not lose yours.
Matthew 10:42
My followers post photos of
SantaCon in town and
A holiday hoedown in the city.
But
On the 10th day of Christmas
NBC gave to me news that
The body of a 7 year old illegitimate child
Was found dead in custody.

The concept foreign to my ears.
I cannot stomach this reality.
I squeeze my Jesus piece for comfort.
But all I can hold is my breath.
She died of dehydration.
The idea of illegal aliens
Still alien to me.
Since when
Did Prisoners of war
Get better treatment
Than little rascals?
In seeking asylum
She stumbled into Heaven instead.
After a journey of over 3,000 miles
I hope she replenishes
In the Fountain of Youth.
Because a cup

Of water in the custody
Of border patrol
Is apparently
Too much to ask for.
I ask for forgiveness

For every thought
Currently filling
My mind.
Everything in my heart
Is raging.
Overflowing
Like the seven seas.
Ready to flood
The world so adamantly,
Not even an arc
Noah assembled
Would suffice.

This my flash flood warning.
I have the fury
Of a parent
Forced to bury their child
Cradled in my fingertips.
I made the grave mistake
Of having a daughter
In America.
When this is no place
For little girls.
But there is no place
Safe for little girls
kissed by the sun.

Jakelin Caal Maquin

Was no older
Than the wine
In a cellar.
Jakelin Caal Maquin.
Tried to escape poverty
But got caught on the
Barbed wire of
A dictator's tongue.

Jakelin Caal Maquin.
Will be left in God's hands
Because ours were too incompetent
Upholding the law
Instead of holding up the weary.
Jakelin Caal Maquin
Takes with her
Hopes of a better tomorrow,
While armrest activists
Conclude history repeats.

Jakelin Caal Maquin
Was excited to
Have the chance
Of owning her
First toy in America.
I wonder how long
It will take
Before we own up.

Jakelin Caal Maquin.
Say her name
Until it becomes a chant.
In a nation full of deaf ears
I feel a Tidal wave of emotion.

Meanwhile,
This country has done everything
To stop the flow of unwanted immigrants.
The Statue of Liberty
Has led us on a suicide mission.
She says,
"Give me your tired.
Your poor.
Your huddled masses
yearning to breathe free.
Send these,
The homeless,
The tempest-tossed to me."
We did.

These Central Americans
Had better odds in a blender.
They have been
Tear gassed.
Arrested.
Starved.
Raped.
And murdered.
How many inexplicable deaths does it take
To get to the beginning of a
Revolution?
I'm wearing all black
On this brown skin.
White chalk outlines hug
The bodies of my people
Longer than their parents.
Thinking of sealing every chimney
To prevent Christmas from coming.
If caravans are not welcome,

Neither is Santa.
Lips of citizens that speak ill of refugees
Are just as lethal as the force used
At the border.
Borderline Christians
Who can celebrate
The holiday of a refugee
But disparage the
Welcoming of refugees
Should be denied entrance
Into the same Kingdom
They seek.
I hope their
Stockings overflow
With coal.
This cold world
Feels more like the
North Pole
More than it does
North America.

How many Americans
Will use the services of an immigrant
During the most wonderful time of the year
But rebuke the conversation of them
At the dinner table?
Will allow their nanny to pick up their kids
From private schools?
Decorate their tree
With nutcrackers?
Perfectly starch their clothes
For minimum wage
To be worn at
An ugly Christmas sweater party

While the ugly truth remains.
The color of your skin
Can and will be used
Against you.
Against all odds,
My people STILL march on.

My daughter asks me to read her
Favorite bedtime story:
The Polar Express.
But after every page I turn,
I can't help but think
Of The Little Engine That Could.
If Jakelin's last thoughts were:
For I was hungry
And you gave me hate.
I was thirsty and
You gave me death.

That's what our actions said.

It is impossible to worship
The child born in the manger
While turning
Our backs
On the child found dead
In custody.
May we live by our crosses
Like we kill for our flag.

Community garden

Nia,
I wish you were blowing out candles on your cake
Instead of our community decorating
MacArthur Station
For your birthday.
I wish
Your sister had a pocket full of posies
To ward off the plague that is fast on our heels.
I wish
Your pit stop did not become your
Resting place.
That you could have grown into the bouquet
Your parents foresaw when
They become florists.
That I didn't have this seed of doubt
Every time that my daughter wants to take
Bay Area Rapid Transit.
I wish
Anytime we touched the Rail
your name and Oscar Grant's did not
Leave such a bitter taste in
Our alimentary canal,
But instead
Served testimony
As the light at the end of the tunnel.
I wish people knew in Swahili
Nia means purpose.

But according to KTVU
You were more suspect than victim.

Which is why
I suspect they aired an image of you
Brandishing a gun when in reality,
Everyone in the station should've been
pistol-whipped
For thinking that made you more of a threat.
Because you can never be unarmed when
Your skin is the weapon.

I wish
we had a crumb of comfort
Knowing your culprit
Was looking at life,
But we stopped looking
Through rose-colored glasses
A long time ago.
A meadow full of white lilies lay at the
Feet of your memorial.
If it wasn't for all the sweat and tears
That went into their formation,
I think we woulda ran lighter fluid
Over the Bart tracks
And burned this town down by now.

The West Coast showed strength in numbers
The week following your passing.
I scrolled through Twitter
The night of
when I was on the East Coast.
Saw enough hashtags to indicate
There was a new headstone
In our field of unfulfilled dreams.
No wonder kids in Oakland stop believing in
fairytales.

The stench of strange fruit greets us
Before we ever have a chance
To wake up and smell the daisies.

Days don't get easier.
We just grow thorns.
I was a weeping willow
When I finally decided
to pay a visit to your altar.
In an alternate universe
You'd be courtside watching the warriors
Instead of Steph Curry paying respect to you
Through a charity game.
It feels like a bad version of
Musical chairs.
Every step similar to
dragging my toes in quicksand.
We getting picked off 1-by-1
But grief and music
Go hand in hand.
And instead of us swinging back
We tweeting out.
There's a handful of Nias
That didn't get to blossom.
Plucked from the soil.
Blown out before they ever had
The chance to wither.
Their aspirations
Gone with the wind.
I never thought I'd
See the day
Black girls
Would become
Dandelions.

G.O.A.T.

You grew up in a city
that is more known
for gangs than tennis.
You leave behind
a legacy of
toughness and
a family dynasty
that'll never be duplicated.

But if you look closer
Under the fine print
you'll see the footprints
of every child in braids and beads
that ever picked up a racquet and
walked onto a court
in a black one shoulder mini,
complete with a tulle tutu
layered with elastic bike shorts
who flirted with the idea
for just one match,
they were you.

You were straight outta Compton.
Straight from the pages
of Sports Illustrated.
In the body issue of
ESPN.
the cover of Time.
the face of Vogue.
gracing Vanity Fair.

GQ's woman of the year.
If Black girl magic
had its own
constellation
it would orbit Venus.

Perfectly Serena
in your bantu knots
or head wrap
from teen Vogue
to Ebony
You are the Essence of
strength and beauty.

WIMBLEDON OWES YOU AN APOLOGY.
The world owes you an apology
for every double standard
you ever competed against
but never redeemed the points for
in your box score.
For every umpire
that ever endured a
string of obscenities
from a male player
and only
issued a warning,
but stole
a point from you
for violating the code of conduct.
You deserve a coat of arms
for your heraldry.
For calling out sexism
in the same breath
that you called match point.

For smashing
patriarchy on its head.
For rallying from a
pulmonary embolism.
Not even arteries and veins
blocked by blood clots
could prevent you from
driving your case
as the
Greatest Of All Time.

For all 23 times you raised
the coveted women's single trophy
in spite of every single
article in the media
that for the better
part of a decade
has dissected you.
For every time
your body's been attacked
but it's really been
about your Blackness.

For every time you
were scrutinized mercilessly
for your stature,
towering over your
opponents like a 2 story building,
your greatness too large
to fit in a Barbie house.
For every time you've been
a caricature
and not a synagogue.
How we should be

so lucky to worship your temple.
instead of defacing your shrine.
How you shine in spite of
the disrespect hurled,
providing sanctuary for Black women
grappling with their womanhood.

For being called ghetto
by commentators
because you crip walked on air
after you won a gold medal.
Where were they
when a peer of yours,
Caroline Wozniacki
stuffed her bra
and shorts
to imitate you?
Oh that's right. Laughing.
Like the crowd.

'Cause it's sport to dehumanize
a Black woman's body.
It's hilarious to poke fun
at someone breaking
records and barriers in the same swing.
'Cause the policing of a Black body comes
gift wrapped in this country
in a triad from hell:
racism,
misogyny
and transphobia.

And although you've
beaten Maria Sharapova

17 times in a row,
you still make 1/2
as much as she does
off the court.

You.
constantly
facing full court pressure.
none of your accomplishments
add up to the broad malice
you've had to endure.
your humanity,
constantly denied.
your catsuit
at the French Open,
denied.
you can take the
superhero out of her costume
but you can never take
away her superpowers.

The biggest takeaway is this:
You will never resemble
what the game's upper echelon
say a female tennis
champion should look like.
But ever since you stepped
on the U.S. Open scene
you opened up the gates
for kids from Compton
to Long Beach
to dream
as big as the palm trees
that surround them.

And for the youth
on the other
coast in Bed Stuy
and Queens
to find the queen
within themselves.

Around the world
we've all witnessed
you update the
rulebook
and rewrite the
history books.
GAME.
SET.
MATCH.

Hip Hop don't love you

I record my daughter
Doing the "In My Feelings" challenge
On top of our makeshift dinner table.
Serving per usual.
Rosy cheeks congruent to her blistering sweat.
She goes 0-100 real quick.
Giving a max
Effort for OVO records.
I wonder if she goes this hard for her art class we
pay tuition for.
I know the answer.
"Kiki, do you love me..."
Echoes in the apartment chambers
On repeat.
A part of myself
Wants to sing along with her
The other wants to tell her
That Hip Hop does not love her.

She asks
Why I stop it halfway.
I have not lied to her yet
But I explain in the best way
She is
Not old enough for the content.
Hip Hop
Is more rated R than kid friendly.
BEATS headphones
Do not fit her tiny head
The way Disney ears do.

But as much as I
Want to stampede her
With good music
I don't want to leave a scar.

Since she's mature
Enough to know
My last breath
Might be the
Breaking news
On CNN,
I let her break out
Of a body that is
Constantly under
Surveillance.
I don't always follow
Proper etiquette
But she's fully aware I can dish
Her some real talk anytime.
Anywhere.

I put the breaks
On the song when
It takes a sexist turn
Into obscenity boulevard.
Where four and five letter
Words are
Dropped louder than bombs.

Her seventh birthday is
Around the corner
So I ease her
Down the yellow brick road
Of the rap landscape.

Or maybe I am holding her back
From a storm of expletives.
I want to save her self-esteem
For a rainy day.

Temporarily shielding
Her from words
I know she will hear
On the playground
But under my umbrella-eh-eh
Or at least on my watch
I am slowly
Integrating rap into her lifestyle
The same way Blacks
Inched into traditionally White schools
In Mississippi.
Except I don't want to miss a beat.
Watching each foot so I don't misstep.

I don't want her to discover
That the M in EMCEE
is for misogyny.
And Hip Hop
Is almost inseparable
From chauvinism.
Yet there is a delicate
Complexity in being
A woman
For the culture
Because
It is always undeniably
At the expense of her.

I don't want to
Drizzle on her parade
But the lump sum
Of the billions
The industry rakes in
Is because my favorite rapper
Makes it rain.

That the degradation
Of her very being
Is how they sustain
Their millions.

I know her innocence
Is vulnerable at this age
And the genre
That we go hyphy to
Is vulgar
I am walking a
Tight rope
So I keep
Rappers who
Brag about full clips
And red bones
Out of the playlist.

But no matter
How much parental control
I keep
And as much as she's bopping
Her head to
The instrumental as a toddler,
I know years from now
As a teenager she'll be

Grappling with the lyrics.
I don't want to kill her vibe
But the violence
Against women in the
Music I listen to
From 2pac to Too Short,
Is inexplicable.

And if I could forgo
All of the songs
That have the word
Bitch in them
Then I wouldn't
Have any Hip Hop
To listen to.

I am not riding a
Wave of righteousness
But I'm just trying to
Be more conscious
Of how I raise daughters.
I'm a surrogate to hundreds
Whether or not
That was the objective
But the music I introduce
Them to can be therapeutic
Or have Titanic effects.

I want her to have a sweet tooth
For a rapper's delight
Put some flavor in her ear
So when I'm not around she'll
Jump around
Jump jump

Jump around
In our living room
And pretend I am right there.
I wanna teach her that
Knowledge Reigns Supreme
Over Nearly Everyone
and to listen for the sound of da police

I want her Raising Hell
Like N.W.A.
Nahla With Attitude.

And unafraid to
Fight the power
Fight the power
Fight the powers that be
But I don't want her to be
Down with O.P.P.
Like she's down with
Herself.
She deserves to be
Paid in full.

I wanna be next
To her
When Jesus walks.
So when it's time for her
To drop me off at
The crossroads
It'll feel the same way it did when
I held her hand down the crosswalk.
And hopefully
We'll have more songs
We danced on tables to

Than regrets.
So I can't
Practice one thing
And preach the other.
Ain't no half-steppin
In my neighborhood.
I'm raising a rebel
Without a pause
And the hardest lesson
Is that all that California love
Ain't good for her.
But the choice is hers.

When people ask her
When did she fall in love
With Hip Hop
I want her to say....
U.N.I.T.Y.
'Cause she was first
Introduced to the Queen
So she could see all that
power in herself.
I want her to know
That womanhood
And girl power
are way more important
Than if
She was riding
For a man named Aubrey.

I was born a sinner,
the opposite of a winner,
And I was raised in a culture where
C.R.E.A.M. get the money

Where women were called
bitches and hoes,
And lots of ladies loved this cool J
Oh how I used to love her though.

But now I am a father.
I've turned over a
Whole new leaf.
And her name is
Nahla.

The Marathon Continues

I'm from a place where
Hyphy is religion.
Where we grow our dreads
Just so we can shake 'em.
Where we speak on it
'Cause we got a
Golden State of Mind.
We living in a dope era
No B.C. but on G.O.D.
Oakland and San Francisco
Have been in the blues
Like Crenshaw
ever since you left.
But we know dedication is
Hard work plus patience.
We also know some stars
Who aren't meant to burn long
But they light shines on forever.

Before I left the house
I hugged my daughter
Like I would never see her again.
Before I leave this world
It will know my poetry
It will know my pen
Like it did
Your music
and the last time
That I checked you was
Still the street's voice

Out west.

If you got a lighter or
A phone with a flash
Raise it
Black love
Brown pride
Can we finally embrace it?

If you ever lost somebody
Take a second to reconnect
Summon them
In your hearts and minds
Let them share this space with us

And remember if you
Believe in unity in our community
Black love
Brown pride
Let me show you how I embrace it.

Rest In Power
Nipsey.

Clean water

Alexa
Tell me the last time
Flint had clean water.
She plays a song
"Clean Water"
By Joss Stone
From the album ironically titled,
"Water For Your Soul."
I am not surprised.
How would a
Smart speaker
Know how
To hack the hood?

It is always easier
To face the music
Than the facts.
The people
Of Flint
Have been without
Clean water in their
Pipes for more than
2,015 days
And counting.
Counting on nothing
Short of a miracle.
It is likely every single
Kidney and
Liver,

Have been contaminated.
I hope the people
Of Flint voted
During midterms
Like their lives
Depended on it
Because they do.

General Motors
Stopped using
The water years ago
Because it corroded
Engine parts.
I wonder what
That water does to
The motor skills
And body parts.
I wonder how many
Bath tubs are filled
With clumps of hair.
How many shower
Singing sessions
Have been
Indefinitely postponed
Because mouths
are clamped
Shut
Due to what pours
Out of the shower heads.
How often brown skin
Breaks out
In a furious rash.
Hard to be rational
When our children

Have to brush their
Teeth with bottled water.
They already have every
Obstacle to success
In their path.
Now
The liquid they depend on
For survival
Can have
Fatal consequences
If not boiled at the right temperature.
How does that not dampen their spirits?
My blood boils because this
State of emergency has
Been swept under the rug.
Tossed aside like them.

Intellectual Disability
Is only one of the many
Harmful Effects.
The lead courses through
The water
Spreading
Across the terrain
Like a thief
In the night.
Dreams ransacked
By the government.

A study found
That children under five
Had elevated
Lead in their blood.
Blood is on the hands

Of every city official.
Let April 25th, 2014
Be remembered as the
Day Flint was sentenced
To death by lethal injection.

The day E. Coli and
Coliform Bacteria
Made its debut from every
Faucet.
Where the tap
Started to smell
Like a public pool
And taste like copper.
We've been tap dancing
Around the truth.
That we have a third world
Issue in the
7th largest city
In Michigan.

Up to 60%
Of the human
Adult body
Is made of water
Which tells me
A basic human right
Has been neglected
And negligence
Of that size
Is nothing short
Of genocide.

No arrests have been made

For foul play
But the stories of
Cardiac arrests
Have been
Playing on repeat.
Justice
Skipped over.
Overlooked like the
Majority Black city.
Where 40%
Of people live in poverty.
The soundtrack of
Environmental racism
Is certified platinum.
Just like the H2O.
The life expectancy
For people in Flint
Is 20 years shorter than
People in
Neighborhood suburbs.
Now that they have to
Choke down lead-laced water.
I doubt that
Increases their chances.

For all intents and purposes
We didn't
Drop the ball.
We released
A nuclear bomb.
Transforming
Flint into
The Stone Age.
It's hard to wash

My face in the morning
Without thinking of the
Worst man-made catastrophe
Happening to
People who got
Separated after
The diaspora.
It hits close to home.

I ask Alexa to play some
Motown music
To drown out the thoughts
But the toxic effects
Of what's happening in
Flint makes my eyes water.
And tears runs
Down my cheek
And onto my lips
As salty they are,
I can't complain.

I could have the taste
Of a cold metal coin
On my tongue.

Poisoned soil

Kevin Hart said
One of his biggest fears
Was his son growing up and being gay.
And I wholeheartedly understand that.

Stand up and Hip Hop
Have always had a lot in common.

How your son identifies
Is far worse of a reputation than
A baby being born with
Cerebral Palsy or Down Syndrome.

The greatest sin
Homosexuality
Still carries a lifetime ban,
Non-exempt
During family holidays.
Gayness
The most heinous crime
One can commit
Grants you an non-refundable
Ticket to exile.
Ascribing to any letter
Of the LGBTQ community
Automatically condemns you to hell.

Unless you are willing
To repent
Or be DELIVERT

You cannot sit at the master's table
With child predators
And pedophiles cloaked
In catholic clothing.
Father forgive them.
They know not what they do.

If I could write a letter to my
12-year-old self I would say:
When they call you a faggot
Do not respond.
When they ask you to
Play smear the queer
Walk the other way.
When they label you a girly man
Take it as a compliment.

Do not let this world
Turn you into a monster.
The boogeyman
Is not under the bed
It is in the undertone of society
That sends men running from the
Closest association to the divine feminine.

Mr. Hart,
I know you're in the funny business
But if your son comes out
I hope you are more
Trampoline
Than bed of nails.
A parachute
For his landing
And not the

Noose for his neck.

I hope behind closed doors
If he leaves the closet
You are a welcome mat.

I hope if he ever
Tells you he's curious
You do not view his orientation
As a sickness
That can be cured by holy water
And Hail Marys.

That who he sleeps with
In the same bed
Will not affect
The family inheritance.
That if he decides
To enroll in the armed forces
and
Don't ask, don't tell
Is not still a policy
I hope he has the courage
to walk in his light or
walk away.

Hate crimes have risen
For the third straight year
In the United States
And although I do not
Identify as a member
Of the LGBTQ
I am an ally.

The only thing worse
Than having to bury
Your seed
Is being dead to them
Before they ever hit
The ground.

I am standing on poisoned soil.

It is still easier
To have an open carry license
Than
Be openly out.

The Moscone-Milk Assassinations
happened at City Hall
Before I was born
And every night
I go past the buildings
As they light up I wonder
Do they even know that
Decades later their souls
Are a lighthouse
For all the homeless
LGBTQ transitional age adults
Who have been cast ashore.

And since they make up the largest demographic
Without a roof over their head
I'd rather not be lukewarm
About the issues
Affecting my community.
I've gotten cold feet

For my beliefs before.
Never again.

I will be no bystander
In this apocalypse.

And if my daughter ever
Came out to me
I'd love her just as much
As she did the moment
She came out the womb.

Mija

Mija.
You have a story.
It is written all over your brown skin.
The latest fashion trend
Is not a result of
Cosmetic surgery.
Your golden bronze requires no Maybelline
To shine any brighter
Than it already does.
That coat passed down
Generation after generation
Has been worn with the pride of a people,
Who like the land they inherited,
Was ripe with ancestral knowledge.
Whose resilience
Knows no border.
Deeply sown into the
Fabric of your being
There lies a warrior.
Translation:
You got, you got
Greatness
In your DNA.

Being Native
Was not a card you had a hand in
But you have played with
A poker face
That has left opponents
Constantly asking you to

Cater to their discomfort.
Smile more.
Look less angry.
Caught in-between society norms
And gender roles.
Your next move
Always their greatest concern.

If the Spanish of your tongue
Alarms the monolingual,
Do not cover your accent in apology.
Lo siento, no lo siento.
Let your rolling r's
Flow like a raging river.
Remind them
Bilingualism is a
Superpower.

You can raise
Hairs on the
The backs of necks
And every conjugated verb
That leaves the surface of your lips
Is a reminder
To the elite who hate the use of our
Native tongue,
That this country was built on
Our backs.
The extreme heights of your potential
Combined with the
Rising voice
Of your generation
Has those in power
On the ropes.

They want to separate our families
Because the ground beneath them
Is shrinking.
The homosapians are running.
Are aware their power
Is dying off
And in their wake
You will take their place
At the top of the totem.
And that is
A lasso of truth.
And although DC comics never got the wave,

You.
More Wonder Woman,
Than damsel in distress.
Are the synonym for chingona,
Fearless.
Did you know
The blood of the Aztecs
Courses through your veins?
You are a mean, bleeding Latina.
Your train of thought
Has indigenous origins.
You are a departure
From the norm.
The only thing ordinary about you
Is how you're able to be
A chameleon for people.
Blending in to protect your identity
When in reality
Mujeres fuertes like you
Start revolutions
By solely existing.

It is a fiesta
From the cradle
To the Quinceañera
And every moment after
You live la vida loca.

Mírate.
Your Frida flower crown
And big hoop earrings.
The only armor you need.
History does not honor you
The way you deserve.
You have a story.
It is written all over you.

Mija.
Write your
Name amongst the stars
Where it rightfully belongs.

Mija.
Escribe tu nombre entre
las estrellas.

Class full of incredibles

I spoke to a class full of
Incredibles
Disguised as 5th graders
After introducing them
To spoken word
I gave them a handwritten prompt:

IF YOU HAD ANY SUPERPOWER WHAT
WOULD IT BE?

I, 20 years their senior
Could not imagine
The schooling I'd be in for
That morning
Their minds
Packed like I-405
Began to haul in heavy thoughts
I saw the wheels moving
But was not ready for
The rush hour ahead.

Ahead of their time
They took me on
A high-speed chase
An accomplice to their brilliance
Them, radiating with the
Authenticity only a child can offer
Ready to take me to
Churcccch

During school hours.
One after another they
Filed up like
Public attorneys ready
To give a hearing
Prepared to testify
Ready to tell the truth.

THE.WHOLE.TRUTH.AND.NOTHING.
BUT.THE.TRUTH.

They could of given a tutorial
On public speaking but
As they spoke truth to power
All I could do is marvel
Personalities larger than infinity
With one snap of their finger
They'd be able to eliminate
1/2 of the universe's problems.

One said they'd
Bring the world
Peace and joy
By dancing.
I instantly imagined her
Harlem-shaking
Things up in our government
Doing the reject in
The East Wing
Creating a rapid
Rotating column of air
Strong enough to blow
Away anti-immigrant rhetoric
Her poof balls

In all their splendor while she
Performs the Macarena
At the State of the Union Address
Capitol Hill on happy feet
As she, in her multilingualism,
Leads us into a new day
Past her curfew
As we dance with the stars.

Another said they'd move
Mexico right in the middle
Of the United States so
There'd be no reason for a wall
Little did he know
Texas, Arizona, New Mexico, California
and his hometown were all states
That belonged to it.
Little did I know empathy
That large could fit into the body
Of a 10 year old
His heart already larger
Than the Grinch's
After it grew three sizes
Taught me the
True meaning of courage
His strength in his face of pain
Made me want to look into his future
And see the mountains he'd move.
On top of them, heavenly terrain
The ones a king dreamed of
The ones my grandmother hoped for
The one I have dedicated my life to finding
When we say the youth is the future
This is what we mean.

Another said they'd
Wave a magic wand and turn
Hate into love
And fear into confidence
She, in that moment,
Was the living embodiment
Of Mother Teresa
Nobel Peace began with her smile
Restoration left her lips like a
Hummingbird
Traveling 49 miles per hour
Her words like sweet nectar
Left every educator
In the room
Teary-eyed
And eyes wide open
At the same time
Because the innocence
And intuition of a child
Is something
We'll never have again.

And in my chair
I morphed from
Well-seasoned adult
Into an infant who
Forgot how to speak
Choked up with emotion
Cause I knew of a tent full
Of children their age
In shoes their same size
On the other side of the border
Who desperately needed that wand
Who grew up

Being taught survival
And as they seek asylum
Have no idea
There are superheroes
Their age who exist.

Morena magic

Congress Woman Alexandria Ocasio-Cortez:
I stayed up past my curfew
To watch you on the
Light night show with
Stephen Colbert.
I haven't been that
Starstruck since I saw
J. Cole in concert.
You were soul food
that MLK day
And ironically
You were a testament of hope.
And every time you spoke,
It reminded me
Why we can't wait.

I been doing my
Best to watch my weight
But after you busted open
Some Ben & Jerry's
Live on air
I called an Uber
to get my own pint of
Americone Dreams.
But then I cancelled.
'Cause the CEO supports
The current admin,
And I'm in no business
Of funding hate speech
So I put my money

Where my mouth is
And called LYFT
While I thawed out.

I know you got
A handle on Twitter
And a strong following
I been considering
Reactivating my account
But the way my AT&T plan
Is set up I'm all out of data.
You fired on all cylinders
When you had
Mark Zuckerberg
From Facebook
On the hot chair.
It's not every day
Billion dollar businessmen
Melt into a Dublin mudslide
But I can admire
A good grill session.

Growing up I heard
A woman's place
Is in the kitchen,
But you've been
Re-writing the narrative
Ever since New York
Placed you in the
House of Representatives.
You been reppin for
Every Latina with
the gold hoops
And red lipstick.

I know Sonia Sotomayor
Slammed the gavel,
Voters from the
Bronx to the Bay
Hit the Quan
Whenever we
See you stand for democracy
Or dance like the
GOP is watching.

I know the Obamas
Cautioned you to
Stick to more neutral colors,
But if you ain't been neutral
on the side of injustice
I doubt you'd camouflage now.
Redressing our grievances
Without gender conforming.
Disrupting the status quo
With the raise of a brow.
And on this Historic wave
illustrating that women
Can wear the pants
And stunt in pantsuits.
Serving looks and policy
change at the drop of a dime.
Surround by snakes in disguise
With prehistoric views
That white out our voices
And paint us as vermin

But your
Morena magic
has been cleaning

Out the cabinet
Since you were sworn in.
And I swear
When I was window shopping
I saw that you'd been
Transformed from
A Congresswoman
Into comic book anthology.
I held the graphic novel
Of a bartender turned
Superhero in my hand...
And thought of my grandmother
Who I'd of FaceTimed that sec
If my iPhone had a signal
To reach the pearly gates
And she'd of seen the
Tears of joy
Running down my cheeks.

Cause I remember
how she cried like a
Newborn and lost her voice
When she saw
the presidential inauguration
of a former
Senator from Illinois.
Then I thought
5 years from the present,
In the year 2025,
What my daughter
Will say about me
When we're watching the
Inauguration of our
Country's first female president.

White lies

I wonder
When I see
A white woman
In passing why
I smile
To let them know
I come in peace.
But a piece of
My dignity dies
In every inch of my
Non-genuine crease.
Why my lips flinch
To let them know I am safe.
To let them know I mean no harm.
I mean
I wonder
If they sniff
My fear
Like great white sharks smell blood
In the water?
I wonder if they are aware
They can make an orphan
Out of my daughter.
Make me shark bait.

I wonder if they realize
One white tear
Is worth my whole life?
If my discomfort is obvious.
I wonder if they know

A little white lie
Has the power to
Separate neck from body,
Turn decadent limbs
Into strange fruit,
Leave family trees
hanging from words
Without legal trial
Make scarecrows
Out of Black souls
I wonder
Why a chill runs down my spine
When we share the same sidewalk
And they clutch their bag
Like I'm the big bad wolf

If they know how
Many Black boys I know
Tremble in they shoes
When a white girl cries wolf.
Makes werewolves
Out of black skin.
Hunted down with
Silver bullets
And white-masked men.
Carrying crosses
On Sunday mornings
And burning them after service.
That work as our
Policemen
Judges
And doctors.
How many nominations
Did Ava receive

For recreating New York's
Central Park 5?
I guess they see us
When we winning emmys
Not when we inmates.

Or maybe it's
All in my head.
I should
GET OUT more often
But ever since
Jordan Peele got US
out of the sunken place
I been seeing
A lot more skin folk
Than ain't Kinfolk.
Now I'm the one
walking around with mace.
Trying to breathe,
Stretch, Shake, Let it go
But I can't Harlem Shake
The fact that Emmett Till
Had to meet his maker
Before he ever
Had a chance
To grow facial hair.
Why the white woman
Who accused him
Of winking went
6 full decades living
The American Dream.
Before she published the truth
At her deathbed.
I wonder how many

Rose petals
Have been laid
On the ground
For Rapunzel.
Or Caroline.
Or Amanda.
Or how many men with melanin
Gotta go 6 feet deep
Before we are on the
Endangered list.

We must be kin
Of the Black rhinoceros
But the true irony is
the most popular viagra pill
On the black market is called rhino.
That white men
Are most responsible
For purchasing.
Why they boner seem
to last a lot longer
Than our lifetime.
You know the word
orgasm
In French
 is pronounced
"Le petit mort"
Meaning the mini death.
But do you know what
The safari and USA
have in common?
They hunt for sport.

I been a trophy
For far too many walls.
A notch on the belt
Of white girls
Who fetishize
Black features
And fantasize
About the way my
Boa constricts.
Shedding all beliefs.
Who hated they family morals
But loved the way I
Pinned they body
Against dry paint.
As if that was the only
Time they ever felt
Like a masterpiece.

I wonder if my
Ancestors ever
Knelt before theirs
And whispered
"Oh yessa massa"
On bloody knees.
Why the most common
Pick up line
From a white woman is
"We'd make some
cute light skin kids?"
Why they want a weapon they
have no idea how to wield?
Why Goldilocks
Get to break and enter
And still wave the victim flag?

But the older I get
I can relate grizzly familiar
To the 3 bears.

Most important question
Worth asking is...
Why is
Becky with the good hair
Who ain't no good for me
Make my hair raise
and I can't help but stare?

Pages of my story

In this pursuit
Of happiness
I am more Chris Gardner
Than Will Smith.
And since I'm on the
Same soil where
Fortune cookies are made
I know the answers
Are stuffed inside.
So even if I crack
Under pressure or
Fail to make the Fortune 500

I'm willing to surf on couches
As a middle aged man
To preserve these
Childhood dreams.

There are too many adults
Holding on by a thread,
Painting a smile on
their 9-5,
Counting down
To retirement.
I know plenty of artists,
Those starving
And eating seconds
Who power nap in their car
Get up and go after
What fuels them.

And I rather leave my dreams
On earth next to them
Than take my ambition
To the graveyard
That is already overpopulated.

I never imagined
I'd even make it to
32
Much the less
Tour the country.

Show after show
Sleeping
In time shares on the road
Then waiting to hear back
From friends in the Bay
With last minute notice
If I'll nap on a park bench
Or on their apartment floor.

I can't complain
About a night's rest
On a hard floor
When people my age
Haven't even reached the conclusion
Regarding what's worth going hard for.

Got a duffle bag
With clothes to
Last a full week.
Spent too many
Years half-stepping
What I loved doing

For jobs that
I busted my ass for.
If I had dropped dead
From health complications
I'd be replaced
Within a work week.
My daughter
Whose imagination
Is bigger than
The circumference
Of my city
Says when she
Grows up
She wants to
Be like me.

I'd hate for her
To graduate
College without a job
Be swimming in debt
Floating around
Part time
Until she discovers
Her purpose.
But then again,
There is a fearlessness
I live with
Unparalleled to anything
She knows.
She must see that
Resiliency is my signature.
Maybe she feels
The pulse of life
In my penmanship

From every postcard
She hangs on her door.
How each zip code is different
But I am the same man
She's known from birth.
That her father
Has been under
The Eiffel,
And simultaneously
Crumbled
Like the twin towers
In her lifetime.
Has created a living
Writing her name
In the pages of my story.

That people have grown
Up with her in my
Self-published works.
So in many ways
Although she is an
Only child
My readers are more siblings
Than consumers.
She is the fruit of my labor.
Will reap what I sow.
And If I gotta exist
Some time between places
That is a price I
Am more than willing
To pay.

Bay Area Renaissance.

Tongo Eisen-Martin,
American book award winner asks me
When I arrive to Litquake
A quarter late
Where are the rest of my clothes.
I came in my signature short shorts
and a tank top
In the middle of October.
I thought I told someone
A long time ago to
Please get they uncle.
I got a blunt rolled and I'm featured next door.
I came ready to light that joint up.
Sharing the stage with Thea Matthews is a
Blessing that such few get the honor of.
The room hot as a sauna
Humidity foggin the windows
You'd think we dipped our afros in soul GLO
Audience patiently waiting.
I can hear a pin drop.
Improv Jav drops me his location.
He's in the Bayview
Of Scam Fran I pull up
With no hesitation.

When Nick Fury hits ya line
You know some avengers assembling.
I share a Lyft with poet laureate Kim Shuck.
She's in her squid vicious hat ready to unpack
an arsenal of metaphors at a marathon

moby dick reading.
She asks me if I know any youth she can
organize a reading series with and I answer
with a smirk.

My phone vibrates. It's a notification from la
Mexicana Sophia.
She just released her second book at 19.
I knew back at Mission High those other
teachers would eat their words,
that Latina with fire is prime evidence
You never lose your fire
By lighting a single match

Can't forget Queen Niya debuting her literary
work as we speak
She got Thanksgiving break next week.
Love when a big girl has big dreams.
Too big to fit on cover folds
Can't wait till she on the cover of Time
The big girl reclamation happening right on cue.
I hook up Shuck with their contacts and
As I jump out my whip I see Paul S. Flores
Waiting for his ride. The Mexican and Cuban
stallion that told a play on the hill of
our fallen soldier Alex Nieto.
Always a blessing when you can move mountains
with a living legend.
I walk in the doors of the Opera House and see
Flavia Elisa Mora telling the story of a
desert flower.
My eyes flow with tears as she paints a portrait
of immigration nearly as vivid as the mural she's
designed on the corner of 24th and Capp.

I dap up Josiah Luis, mi hermano from
another chingona.
I can feel the full-blooded poncho Spanglish-
speaking poet's energy
in my palm of my hand long after our embrace.
He wears the pride of our ancestors all in the
shape of his face
After I rock the mic, Forced to Fly calls me, I
answer in 1 ring,
Before I know, I'm on the run. She's outside
ready to mob across the bridge.
We gotta speak on it. I know it's town biz but
before I leave I let rip an "erray"
so loud you could feel
The tremors all over the bay
After switching lanes we park and walk in,
We don't show ID or pay for entrance.
I look at the stage and I'm in a trance.
The Poetic Pharaoh curating with the
kinda enchantment that'll make you believe
God is a Black woman.
Then before my eyes
A kid from Oakland
Is next on the list
And within seconds
He yells "yeeeeee" and
We all vibrate higher
With the almighty
Plans and desires...
If you ain't know
Upside down ghost go craaazy
You can catch Simba taking
quality pics of the artists,
The Host of the diagnosis,

Ivan Casonova slides next to me,
He letting the beard grow
And as it does his flow surges.
They know after this event
I'm gonna have dibs
On that pull-out futon.
Day lite shoots me a wink
From across the bar.
The talented verbalist
From Vallejo is an inspiration
No matter where she go
So since it's a coincidence we
under the same roof
I order a glass of Blue Moon.

Ton Oliver makes a guest appearance.
He usually on Bart securing the bag.
He one of the most famous
buskers in the land.
Gracing the SF chronicle and KQED.
I'm just happy to catch my
Afro Latino brotha before he
performing on MTV.

Malaysia the co-creator
Of second Mondays
Walks by and gives
My sides a squeeze.
A disciple with the delivery,
No wonder she feel like Jesus.
I bow on my knees and
Kiss her hand in all humility,
Not every day you touch such royalty.
I take a look at my timeline.

See my fraternity brother Prentice Powell
with his kids.
He a hell of a father. But that man move like a
Harlem Globetrotter.
The NAACP image award nominee is probably
the reasonI decided to turn my poetry into
spoken word and
That's word to any emcee that has a dollar
and a dream.
Six Footah The Poet
Commands the space
When Tiffany calls her up.
Can't call the bluff of a poet
That towers over the competition.
She a skyscraper in the Bay and
When she spit, your unborn grandchildren can
feel the words she reverberates.

The night's coming to an end
And Natriece Spicer
Comes to serenade,
BAE is Black and Educated
She reminds me of my Sega Genesis.
And second Corinthians.
And by the end of her piece I'm in 1000 pieces
Before I get called to close
My heart beat out of sync
My hands sweaty like I washed dishes
In the kitchen sink.
I put my head down to pray.
Look up and before I lose all touch,
I realize this is the

Bay Area Renaissance.

Tokyo drift

Disclaimer:
I have
Never been to Japan.
But I am down
To Tokyo drift with you.
Be a total tourist.
Ask locals to take
Photos of us in
Front of cherry blossoms.
So I can turn them
Into seasons greeting cards.
Take enough saki bombs
Before I feel it
Hard enough
To feel comfortable
Bombarding you
With stories of
When I was a youth.

Scale
Mount Fuji.
I hear it has
Inspired artists
And poets
And since we are
Both I figure
We can elevate
Our talents.
I know you are
Not afraid

Of heights
By looking
At your talons.
Besides you have
Enough experience fighting
Uphill battles
For the both of us
So this will be more second nature
than fear factor.
I ain't ever felt
Something this
Organic.

Ever since you swung
My way I have been
More prone
To going with the flow
And nothing says that
Quite like getting a pound
Of Chiquita bananas
And feeding them
To wild monkeys
In Koyoto Park.
And if they take
A liking to you
We can take
A few back
to America.
I am kidding.

Chris Brown
was facing 6 months
In jail
On 2 misdemeanor

Counts of possession
Of an exotic animal
Without a permit.
And I am
Still out on
Bail
And my skin brown
so maybe
karaoke is a safe bet
Unless you want
To sing duets
Then I am
More than willing
To channel
My inner
Lionel Richie.
And go
ALLLLLL night long
Or until we are
Kicked out.
Whichever comes first.
You don't need
To worry about
Cumming last.

I go from
Spoken word artist
To Super Saiyan
REALLLLL fast
Whenever you
Get my
Temperature rising
Like ramen,
Which sounds

Like a nutritious way
To refill your tank
After I fill you
With some vitamin D
When you are on E.

Once the food settle
We can travel
200 millimeters
An hour.
I've never
Taken a bullet
For anyone
But I'd be down to
Board a bullet train
With you.
We can rent
A kimono
And sightsee
Hiroshima
Or rock traditional
Japanese
Ninja clothing
At a dojo
And unleash
The
Dragon.

And since
You have a
Tendency
To breathe
Fire
On the microphone

All over the west coast
I been looking
At round trips
That leave
From Frisco.

I have never
Been to Japan
But I heard
The leaves
Blaze
Red and gold
In autumn
Similar to
My 49ers starter jacket
Or the shades
Of your cheeks
When you blush
When you're anxious.
Ain't it peculiar
That as you've
Been experiencing
Heavy winds
Your flame hasn't
Flickered
But
There's
Lots of
Love
Hotels
Where
Our romance can
Rekindle.
Or set sail.

I can't
Tell you the last
Day I had
The luxury to
Cruise through
But if your
Dreams are big
Enough
Let's take a
ship to
Vancouver.
Where space
And privacy
Are a premium.
But quality time
With you is a luxury
And you look
Like you need
A vacation.
And while we
Are still young
I want to spend
My prime with you.
I rather say
Oh well
Than
What if.

But if
I found some
Cheap tickets
On Trip Advisor
Would you meet

Me at the airport?
I think it's
Worth a LYFT.
Cause I will Pokemon Go
Anywhere
As long as it involves you.
I got this wanderlust
For you.
I'd hate for life
To get away from us
So are you up to
Tokyo drift with me?

The revolution comes with twerking

Someone told me in my DMs
That real men don't twerk
Butt what I do
What my thick thighs
Don't make me hold this head
Any less high.
I remember watching
Prince move his hips
Like there was freedom
In the bones
Controversy
Always a turn away
But his little red corvette
Gave my low rider
The green light to
Defy gravity.

Bouncing this back side
Like it was laced with
Hydraulics
This body contorts
Whenever the beat drops,
A sacrifice for the GODS
And I will present this offering
Every time a DJ spins cash money
Taking over for the 99 and 2000
Something MYSTICAL
About the way I shake it fast,
But watch yourself
Before you

Treat it with contempt.
This temple is an inheritance
of Mapouka.
Which makes me
The beneficiary
Of muscles that can
Bend without breaking.
The vibranium I carry
In this bone marrow
Comes with no return policy.
The West Africa in my back
Cannot be colonized.
So would I like a
shake with those fries?
Yes.

And while I'm at it
Make it super size
'Cause freedom is worth torment.
Like running a marathon
With a torn meniscus
I'll walk if I need
Crawl if I must,
But I won't quit.
Even if I
Encounter hellfire
Or get scalped
At the pulpit.

From the basement parties
In Oakland
To the cathedrals
In the Dominican Republic
If the spirit moves me

I will wobble everything
Beneath my spine.
Unbeknownst to you
I was born a preemie.
So I've been fighting
For my right to be here
Since I was a fetus.
So am I extra?
YES.

And I don't fit.
I've been ridiculed
Since I was in grade school.
Told I couldn't do
do the Macarena
Told men don't shed tears
But my limbs have
Been crying out
Since I fit below
The window seal
And to this day
I still don't know
How to fit under
Anything.

If nothing
My students
Will remember me
As the first male
They knew within reach
To break thru
The glass ceiling of toxic masculinity.
So in touch with my divine feminine side
Mother Nature

Sends her lady bugs
As a gentle reminder
to keep leading a vibrant
And color-full life.

So I'll be damned
If I am a stunt double
To my true nature.
Because this mahogany
can no longer be
Policed, objectified or repulsed
Without my consent.

So anyone sliding in my DMs
insinuating
What real men do
Better know in the time
It took to find fault with my
Self-expression
I've already found grace
In my response.
Better know I understand
How frequently people cope
By what they project...
Better know
I'm subject to pop
Lock and drop
And return
Stronger than ever.

So will the
Revolution come with some
Twerking?
Hell YES.

Cracks in the patriarchy

Michelle Obama's latest memoir
inspired a class curriculum
that seeks to empower
black girls.
I think that's worth
A standing Ovation.
I'm starting a petition
to incorporate that same
course of study
in my daughter's school.
She is American grown,
and although
there are some growing pains,
she sprouts morning glory.
I really like who she's Becoming.
I want her to know she is loved.
I want her to know
why the sun is so quiet,
I want her to know
there may be a reason
she can sow diamonds
in the backyard and her
bowels deliver uranium
the fillings from her nails
are semi-precious jewels
but when she's old enough
I'll just hand her the collected poetry of
Nikki Giovanni
so she can have
cotton candy on a rainy day.

I want her to know that
Poetry is not a luxury.
It is a vital necessity
of our existence.
That we are from a land
where other people live.
And though other kids
On the playground might not
know who Andre Lord is,
She will.
Where else will she
learn that the
master's tools will
Never dismantle
The master's house
and if knowledge is power,
these books be to her
what key be to lock.
I want her to know
The ring of rebellion.
Because your silence
will not protect you.

But the truth will have
her smashing her hooves
through the cracks of
patriarchy like the
Black unicorn
that she is.
I wanna introduce
Her to a Black Panther
who taught
Me violence
Against women

And the ongoing
Challenge to racism.
What's so important
About Blues legacies
And black feminism,
Listen.

I want her to decide
For herself
Are prisons obsolete?
And why DR. Angela
Davis doesn't have
her own holiday.
I want her to know
All my heroes have
FBI records
And that solidarity
Is an action
We live by
and
Not a word
We rehearse
In a spelling bee.
And if they
They come
In the morning
To use her voice
Of resistance
I want her to know
Where we stand.

Class matters.
And the value of
Teaching to transgress

Education as the
Practice of freedom
Because pretty soon
There won't
Be days of the year left
That aren't commemorated
With the fatal shooting
Of a Black body.

And I want her to know
More than a woman's
Mourning song.
And that she
Can lay her hair down
Without putting a
Relaxer in it.
If anyone call her
Buckwheat
I got the
Perfect counterpunch
In her arsenal,
Happy to be nappy.
Courtesy of Bell
Hooks should
Keep her from
Ever having to
Throw in the towel.
And even if
She hits the mat.
You can't keep
A good woman down.

I want her to
Keep absolute trust in the
Goodness of the
Earth.
To become proficient
In taking
The arrow out
Of the heart
Because
That is a skill
I have not
Yet mastered.
And
Memorizing
A periodic table
Doesn't hold
More precedence
Than processing
The secret of joy.

There is a rough
Patch that exists
In the lives
Of everybody.
I want her
To love
The color of
Her skin
Like the color purple.
'Cause I've never
Read a more interesting
Mosaic of women
Joined by their
Love of another,

The men who
Abused them,
And the children
They care for.
Thank you
Madame Alice Walker.

And after all
This reading,
I want great food,
ALLLLLL day long.
And more than
Anything I want to admit
Life doesn't frighten me.
But I am not there.
There is a brave
And startling truth
In acknowledging that.

I stayed up
Till 2 a.m.
Waiting for a
meteor shower
Last night
and I couldn't
Help but realize,
Even the stars look lonesome.
I hope when my daughter
Grows some more,
She'll understand
How filled to the
Brim I was
To pour into such
A phenomenal woman.

I never would of
Picked up a pen
If I never turned a page
Of Maya Angelou.
And I want her to
Know that every thought
I jot down
Feels like a letter
to my Beloved daughter.

Homecoming

I woke up today and
Decided to reintroduce myself
To the world
As Jeremías.
My name had grown
Stale on an identity
That was coming
Out of its cocoon
Pruning these leaves
Behind schedule
I've always been
A late bloomer.
Always been envious
Of names that
Stumbled over tongues
Envious of mis amigos
Whose parents
Immigrated across oceans
That auto-corrected teachers
When they mispronounced their names
so it could fit
Better in their mouth.
Today I want to decolonize
My palate.

I walked down the Mission
District of San Francisco
In search of elote
Or the neighborhood
Paletero man

The scent of carne asada sizzling
And fruta fresca
Permeating throughout
The air.
My lungs fill
With appreciation.
I'm GRATE-FULL
I wore my friend's serape,
Which billowed in the
November wind.
I hear Purple Rain
Pumping out of someone's
Subwoofers
At the intersection.
Which is fitting.
I want to party
Like it's 1999.
I get my second wind.
My favorite color
Is morado,
One of the many things
I inherited from
Mi abuelita.

Her acento
Came separately
But her energía
Flowed thru
My veins
Like her high blood pressure.
Pan dulce no ally for her diabetes
But she always had
A sweet tooth.
Anyone that knows me

Knows how bittersweet
It is to write a poem
In Spanglish.
Knows I have been disowned
Because of mi piel negra.
Knows I used
Either google translate
Or a compañera
To write this poem.
I hope God knows
I tried to right these wrongs
With whatever time I have left.
Heaven knows
I walked thru most my life
Wearing a máscara de Lucha Libre,
Wrestling these Demons
Of not being Mexican enough.
There was no la raza studies
At my 4 year university
But I've learned how to
Recover from the razor's edge
Of exclusivity.
Forgave the Chicanos
That made me feel inadequate
And barrios that called me gringo.
Understood they were only at war
With themselves
And I was caught in the crossfire.

So today cuando salió el sol
En el cielo
And my skin went
From light to copper
When kissed by its rays,

My ancestors must have
Chosen today as good as ever
To light palo santo.
Para salir de la oscuridad.
Emerging from the darkness
I ordered mole from my
Favorite restaurante Mexicano
En Español.
I tipped the trabajador
More than any bartender
I have ever visited.
I got a compliment
On the way out
On my plátano shorts
From someone's tía.
She liked the way
My hips moved to
Cumbia as I paid my bill
She should see
¿Cuántas lamidas toma llegar al centro
de este Tootsie Pop?
Either way.
I am PROUD.
You can hear mi grito Mexicano
All over my sanctuary city
¡Viva La Raza!

I jump on a cable car
To attend one of my student's
Quinceañeras.
I woulda wore
My brown beret
But this Afro
could not be tamed.

I brought her a piñata
Of pinche 45.
Watched mis niños
Make mincemeat
Out of cardboard
And tissue paper.
Wiping tears from my eyes
As I bidi bidi bom bom
To Selena
I bid farewell to
La familia and take
the 49 bus home.
Just in time for a super quesadilla
From El Farolito.
Lately I have found sanctuary
In more taquerias
Than any altar.

I used to pray
Till my knees hurt
For an alternate universe,
One in which I could
snap my fingers
And 1/2 my identity
Would cease to exist.
Black listed from
Family reunions
Because I was the
Black sheep
Made me shed
Association of
Being Biracial
But today I shed
All spells that

Keep me asleep
To my own magic.
Soy un brujo.

Vomiting up all the filth
I was ever told
And 1/2 way believed,
I make space for my wings.
Adding some sabor
To satisfy my midnight munchies
The chile de árbol
Stokes the flame in me.
And although
I am still learning Spanish,
I will not be so easily
Defeated when I mispronounce.
I can't be half anything
When I'm this fully loaded
And on this luna llena
I reclaim my Mexcellence.

I call my friend
Who lets me couch surf
A wave of shame
Begins to leak into me
But I seal it.
Mañana there will
Be children in cages
And a Latina Anne Frank
Hiding from ICE
In an attic
With a diario...
And I hope they find this
Like mariposas find me.

Tea party

I never knew I'd reach the place
Where watching animation movies
Would make me wanna cry.
From Aristocats to Zootopia,
You can see my heart
Breaking on my sleeve.
Girl
You've got me all Inside Out.
Just because I'm known to
rock the microphone
And leave people hanging onto
my each and every word
Like a pair of shoes
Off power lines,
I am no Iron Giant.
In fact
I feel powerless by the hour.

I had a Nightmare Before Christmas
that you were on an episode of
Love and Hip Hop.
I'm still processing that.
It was just yesterday,
I was make-believing
Under pillow forts,
Each rug
Was one command away
From becoming a magic carpet,
And my first crush
Was named Jasmine.

She's got a family now
So it's whatever.
What a Ice Age ago
What a whole new world it is now.
See back in the day,
When I was young,
I'm not a kid anymore...
The most important questions were
What up, Doc?
Or
Who Framed Roger Rabbit?

Now I gotta deal
With a pair of brown eyes,
Asking me,
'What's wrong with Mexicans?'
And
'Who is Tamir Rice?'
I call your grandfather
And hear B.B. King in the background,
Nothing as hard as trying to explain to him
Why his granddaughter cannot play
with a BB gun in the backyard when
her skin is the weapon.

Somedays I wanna be BRAVE.
Somedays I really wanna be Peter Pan again.
Both days I look you square
In your face and remind you
to focus on the Promised Land
before you Hakuna Matata your way
through these divided states.
What an American Tail.
400 years ago

20 of our ancestors were brought here
across the Atlantic against they will
so your lungs know the ocean breeze
far greater than Popeye the Sailor Man
And if your classmates ever tell you that
a Black girl with dreadlocks
cannot be a Little Mermaid
Release the Kraken
Remind them our gills are as
battle-tested as a salmon swimming upstream
And our people know all about
holding their breath under the sea.

See beneath the soil there is substance
Within that Beauty there is a Beast
And before you ever took a step into a
classroom door you already graduated
from Monsters Inc.
You put the magnificent in Maleficent
Even the Boogie Man under the bed
knows better than to start beef.
But if I ever get caught in a stampede
If you're ever craving a fatherly touch
and I'm not within physical reach,
Tilt your head
UP there.
It can be
raining Cats and Dogs or
Cloudy with a Chance of Meatballs
Either way,
like your ANCESTORS
I will be watching over you.

REMEMBER...WHO YOU ARE.

Nahla, remember who you are.

And no
I never taught you
How to Train a Dragon
but you've been a fighter
since your very first hiccup.
Ain't no character from the MCU
can develop half the character you did
when you fought for your life in the ICU

So whether or not you use
your MEGAMIND
Your Happy Feet
or chose to Sing,
there is a world out here mija,
where you can be anything.

We're only here for a
Wrinkle in Time.
These greys
are going by in Turbo mode.
We went from bubble baths
in the kitchen sink to
tea parties where the guest list closed.

101 Dalmatians
Tangled between beanbags
We've got so many Toy Stories.
But Frozen away is
the memory of us
growing old together

And that is a sight worth
melting for.
I never saw the day
talking about animation movies
would make me wanna cry,
but that was before you made
a man outta me.

But I hate to tell you
I'm at war constantly with
my own mind
And fighting my flesh is a
daily chore.
I'm just not trying to
Wreck it Ralph. I just want
to give you the kind of childhood
that you don't gotta spend your
adult life getting therapy for.

So when you wake up tomorrow
and tell me "Daddy,
I wanna be a Good Dinosaur
or a chingona
or a bad mutha...shut your mouth.
BEE it.

Be as THUNDEROUS as the
second you were born.
Be as luxurious as you felt when
we hit that daddy/daughter dance
dripping swag off the arm.
Be Moana.
Be Maui.
But first

Be yourself.
And never let me tell you
what you can't be.

But you are not made of
sugar and spice and everything nice.
You are made of COCO and Kung Fu,
and your old man is a little bit loco
so you mixed with some of that too.
But these are the ingredients of the
Incredibles.
And best believe I reserved the
sweetest parts of myself
for you.

And this dad bod might be out of its prime
But it's still limited edition
with as many features as
Disney Plus
left to Transform
into an auto-bot
with the snap of my wrist
with enough allspark to get you
to the Goodnight Moon and back.
Or to my personal favorite
place in the world...
Infinity and beyond.

Open Mic

In the event of my untimely demise,
Do not demonstrate at the local news station
That decides to use my mug shot
from a decade ago
Instead of the thousands of Facebook profile
photos ever since.

Do not go through my friends' subscriptions on
Netflix
And look at the movies I've previously seen and
judge me.
And finally,
Do not release doves into the sky.

Release poets from their chairs.
Turn my eulogy into an open mic.
Let metaphors and similes sing and
Decorate the sky like fireworks.
At my funeral
I want the magic of spoken word to
Light up the darkness of hearts like fireflies.
Allow goosebumps
To form under the skins
Of attendees
That curate a rise in frequency
From truths birthed in discomfort
That no longer have to be
buried away in anonymity.

I want strangers to find shelter

in the arms of strangers.
I want seeds of exchange
To bloom into a giving tree.
I want it to feel like a fireplace.
I never had one of those growing up.

I want every youth
I ever made a difference in the life of
To have a dance off
kinda like
Michael Jackson's BEAT it video.
I want someone to beatbox
And my closest friends
To display the magic that happens
When men are in a room and can
create lyrics for women
that don't degrade them
or use them as a springboard.

I want it to feel like Spring Equinox.
Everybody at the closest equilibrium.
I want people without homes
to find comfort in my Comfort Inn.
To know there is no crime in being homeless.
There is no sin in needing help.
And the greatest thing you could do in
remembrance of me is
give something to somebody who can't
pay you back.

I want it to feel like Keenan and Kel
when they welcomed a guest into Good Burger.
Can I take your order?
No dress code. Or code of conduct.

May good vibes be the only entrance fee.
I want to hear the trumpets.
And it might not be time for victory
But I want mariachi bands to blare down alleys
Loud enough to make conservatives think
Mexico just took back Cali.

I want some good Mexican food
Served from taco trucks so authentic
that Donald Trump
will want to build a wall the day of.

I then want to hear the national anthem.
I want everybody to take a knee
and look around the room
To see what it's like when nobody has a leg up
on one another.
Post it on social media and tag Colin
with the caption:
#IMWITHKAP

I then want to hear the Black national anthem
I want to lift every voice and sing
Till earth and Heaven ring
I want my daughter
To see the marriage of my culture
The power of being Afro-Latino
Not just the pain.

I want somebody to walk in
Gay or straight and get down on one knee
And request an eternity.
I want Nahla to see love up close.
It has avoided her like the plague

It has avoided her like most Christians at
Black lives matter protests.
Donate 200% inflation of the money I make
Through hard copies and audio books,
To children with speech impediments and
incarcerated parents.

I want everything to tie back to my beginning.
Long after my footprints have faded
I want somebody walking in my shoes
to be able to write a poem with a
smile on their face
Because I would never have done that
'cause understanding was a gift I've been able to
give everybody except myself.

In the event of my untimely demise,
Do not mourn me.
Do not shed a tear.
Instead every Día de los Muertos
Light me a purple candle
and leave me your favorite poem
And I will return facing the rising sun.

Do me a favor.
Keep marching onward and upward
until victory for my people and
Freedom for everybody is finally won.

Testimonies

"Like blues you can't duck or ancestors wandering about the outskirts of a gentrified paradise, Jeremy Michael Vasquez is going in. Past and future meet in his craft like borrowing your great-grandfather's firearm. Wanted posters foreshadowed, we inhabit both crisis and renaissance. Vasquez is the revenge of a thousand slums, our new ritual to come."
—*Tongo Eisen-Martin, Winner of the 2018 American Book Award, a 2018 California Book Award, was named a 2018 National California Booksellers Association Poetry Book of the Year, and was shortlisted for the 2018 Griffin International Poetry Prize.*

"The first time I saw Jeremy Michael Vazquez in art form was at a healing workshop at Saddleback High School. I walked out of that room taller. The second time was at a workshop at Santa Ana College. I walked out fuller. Jeremy shakes the floor when he walks in. He plants seeds in your heart the moment you hear his voice. He has a way of bringing joy and laughter to any dark room and transforming it into a beautiful discomforting experience. So beautiful and raw he leaves you savoring your pain for more. After getting to experience his art form you can't help but to seek for more. Create more. Feel more. Love more. Jeremy is the representation of community unity, love and power. To know him is to free yourself. To know him is to walk louder. And knowing him means loving him."
—*Diana Flores, President, Womxn Empowerment, Santa Ana College*

"Jeremy Vazquez brings an infectious and electrifying energy that resonates with the hearts of the youth. Since meeting Jeremy in 2017, he has conducted healing workshops for over 100 of my students across four schools. I have witnessed the power of his poetry; he heals students and educators in a way I have never seen before. His authentic and genuine spirit liberates others to be courageous and vulnerable to a point where participants confront the root causes of their pain, gain a heightened sense of self, and discover ways to heal. It has been a rejuvenating experience collaborating with an Afro-Latino Bay Area native who incorporates hip-hop pedagogy and poetry to transform the lives of urban youth. You can ask any of the students he has impacted, and they'll let you know he is the real deal."
—*Charlie L Morales, San Jose City College–Adjunct Faculty Member, General Counselor, College Instructor; Skyline College–Hermanos/as Connections to College Coordinator & Instructor*

"As a girl who had lost hope in the education system and in there being any teachers who cared about me and my well being, meeting Jeremy and being able to work with him completely changed my view. When Jeremy came into my 11th grade English class I didn't expect to leave class that day feeling the way I felt, that day I walked out of class feeling liberated of emotions I had been bottling up for months, even years. I felt strong, and valued, and important, and seen. None of those feelings would have been possible without Jeremy, he completely changed my view of my journey

and my struggles and he left an impression on my life that I whole-heartedly believe no one else could have."
—*Camila Estrada, Academy for Careers in Television and Film, Staten Island, New York, Class of 2019*

"Something happens when he walks in the room. The energy shifts. The students know they are in the midst of greatness. He is passionate. His words heal. Students are beyond captivated by what he has to say. His spoken word is a performance of grace and liberation. Jeremy has come to present to students in my class numerous times over the last couple of years. Everyone in the room becomes transfixed. They are completely locked in. He frees up any negativity. He reflects back to the students their beauty and power. I have had many speakers in my Ethnic Studies class over the years, but no one as powerful as Jeremy. Students remember him forever. His words transform and heal. His poetry is like nothing students have ever heard before. They are present in all of it. It is like the words are written for them directly. To experience Jeremy is to be forever changed. And to be honest, every time he comes to my classroom and presents, I too am changed. Unforgettable genius."
—*Carah Reed, Ethnic Studies teacher, Santa Ana High School*

"The day I met Jeremy he introduced himself to me as a healer and a poet. I wondered how in the world that worked out in the real world, but in the last two years I have found out that he is, in fact, both. Jeremy's passion to help youth overcome self-doubt and feelings

of inadequacy and worthlessness is both powerful and effective. His love for the disenfranchised stems from his own life experiences and hardships. He knows the struggles intimately because he has overcome them himself. He is a remarkable man with a message of love and togetherness in the midst of the struggle against corrupt power and endemic racism. His voice is a powerful antidote for so many of the ills of today's world. I invite you to take the medicine he offers, may you experience the healing it will bring."
—*Robert Burroughs, CPA Partner, Genske, Mulder & Co.; member of the Christian organization The Navigators*

"In the little time that I've known Jeremy Michael Vasquez, I've learned three things: He is a very passionate poet, an incredible motivator that anyone could ever have the blessing to know, and he embraces his true self, unafraid to speak his story to anybody. He has inspired and motivated me to be a more positive person. When I first heard Jeremy's poems, I was truly touched in a way that is inexplicable. I was in awe with the incredible man I finally was able to meet. He is my confidant and my inspiration as I keep growing and keep learning in this crazy world!"
—*Grace Marson, Pitman High School, Turlock, California, Class of 2022*

"Jeremy's unstoppable commitment to make a difference in the lives of anyone and everyone he meets—with a keen love for the next generation of our

youth–is deeply infectious and igniting. Over the last year of friendship and collaboration in classrooms and community events, I've witnessed it firsthand: Jeremy's passion to be a truth-teller and hope-deliverer is lighting up the world. This dear brother's mighty heart is propelling him with creativity and compassion into the deep waters of pain in our world…where he's doing something about it. To be sure, the arc of his story is aglow with tangible messages and acts of inspiration, hope, and great big love."
—*Sarah Davison-Tracy, author, speaker, founder of Seeds of Exchange | www.seedsofexchange.org*

"Jeremy has perfected the art of speaking to one's soul. With the blessing of being both Black and Mexican, he is able to easily connect with other people, not because they are the same race, but because they share the same experiences. I had the pleasure of witnessing him in his element when he spoke to high school boys a few months ago. His words, his mannerisms, his insight spoke volumes, giving him such a strong presence, but his act of addressing them as "kings" prompted them to expel emotions they had suppressed for such a long time. It takes a strong person to move people like that. With this experience in mind, I felt compelled to invite him onto my show, Ladies Night Radio Show, where we discussed Toxic Masculinity. The light that drew me to him shined onto my listeners as he dived deep into his experiences a biracial man dealing with feelings that society has told him not to express or discuss. These encounters along with many others helped me

understand how the poet in him emerged and I look forward to seeing exactly how far his legacy will reach."
—*Jackie Martinez, Ladies Night Radio, Los Angeles, California*

"Jeremy Michael Vasquez provides a transformative experience for students every time he steps into our educational space. Even though he is the visitor in our room, he enhances our belonging. His journey becomes ours, no matter our race, ethnicity, religion, orientation, gender, ability, or even age. As we work together confronting the world through his words, we explore external inequities and internal processes. The time spent with Jeremy—with his words, with his presence—is deeply intimate and dynamically collective at the same time. After he leaves, the class reflects that his presence lingers as we continue thoughtfully processing our unique experiences. Jeremy is one person, yet, as he shares himself with us, he reveals a layered complexity. Weeks after Jeremy has spoken, students continue to say, "I'm not the same. I can't go back. I have to go forward." This is the expression of transformation, and it is Jeremy's language of the heart."
—*Anne Steketee, M.Ed., Adjunct Lecturer | Donna Ford Attallah College of Educational Studies, Chapman University; PhD Candidate, Cultural and Curricular Studies, 2020; Graduate Research Assistant | Dr. Tricia Sugita*

"Jeremy Michael Vasquez. When I think of that name, I think monumental, intangible, and an inspiration. When I first met him, I thought—ok nice guy—but, then he started to speak all these powerful words and confidence came right at me. He taught me to love myself when no one else loves you and to be who I am, because I come from kings and queens, and that has inspired me to be the best version of me I can be."
—Kyren Jackson, Century High School, Santa Ana, California, Class of 2020

"The words and works of Jeremy Michael Vasquez transcend all genre, standing alone as dispatches not from a scene, or even a movement, but from an embattled community that has proven time and again its endurance and resistance are not to be taken lightly. His stories blend the core threads of many diasporas into a single tapestry that is raw street knowledge mixed with the greatest impulses of teaching and parlaying wisdom into future generations. There are no words like Jeremy's. No one does what he does, the way he does, so authentically, and you don't need a blurb or a thesis to prove it...just bear witness."
—Paul Corman-Roberts, author of We Shoot Typewriters, co-founder of Oakland's Beast Crawl Literary Festival

"Love, Community, King, are the three words that come to mind when I think of my brother and teacher Jeremy Michael Vasquez. His ability to teach directly from his heart and into the hearts of his students is truly inspirational and moving. Time after time Jeremy has taught and worked with my students in very profound ways, his ability to break through the social barriers we as humans create is amazing to watch. I've seen Jeremy enter a room where students have received him with curiosity and apprehension, and have left my classroom full of appreciation, tears, and love. Jeremy speaks truth to power in a way only possible by someone who has experienced hardship, he speaks and listens from understanding and empathy. Jeremy sees the hearts of my students and connects directly with their souls, I learn so much with how he walks in this world. Jeremy is my friend, and I am a better person because of it. He is truly a powerful educator."

—*Dr. Jorge Facio Rodriguez, Assistant Professor in College of Educational Studies, Chapman University*

Heart of a lion.
Wings of a monarch.
Soul of a continent.
Child of an immigrant.

Who would have thought that a
woman with clipped wings
who migrated here with nothing,
would teach generations how to fly,
communities how to unite,
souls how to light the torches of others,
and a young cub how to be King.

Niccolette Portillo, the artist responsible for the cover art, is straight outta Compton, and currently attends San Francisco State University. She is a queer identifying LATINX who expresses her art through her free spirit and passion.

9 781708 288266